THE PRESS

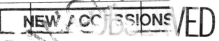

OBSERVED

AND

PROJECTED

EDITED BY
PHILIP FRENCH
AND
DEAC ROSSELL

FILM INSTITUTE

ALSO IN THIS SERIES

A BFI publication produced by the National Film Theatre, London, 1991.

ISBN: 0-851-70-326-7

Typeset, printed and bound by The KPC Group, London and Ashford, Kent

The National Film Theatre, South Bank, Waterloo, London SE1 8XT
The British Film Institute, 21 Stephen Street, London W1P 1PL

INTRODUCTION

This dossier is designed to accompany, amplify, comment on and
ultimately memorialise the two-part season of some sixty-odd
movies dealing with print journalism that we programmed at the
National Film Theatre, London, in July and October 1991 to mark
the bi-centenary of the first edition of *The Observer*, which has been
in continuous weekly publication since late 1791.

Since the 1920s The Observer has taken a serious interest in the
cinema. The paper's first film critic some 70 years ago was the great
Ivor Montagu, life-long Communist, friend of Eisenstein, joint
founder of the London Film Society, producer of Hitchcock's first
comedy- thrillers in the 1930s, scriptwriter-producer at Ealing and
codifier of the rules of table-tennis. He was succeeded by C.A.
Lejeune who remained with the paper until the end of 1960,
sometimes writing her reviews in verse. During her time *The
Observer* presented (in collaboration with the British Film Institute)
the famous "Sixty Years of Cinema" exhibition, devised by Richard
Buckle in 1956. When Ms Lejeune retired the paper published
eloquent tributes to her by Peter Sellers, Michael Balcon and
Anthony Asquith. She was succeeded by Penelope Gilliatt, who
moved to the *New Yorker* in 1967 and scripted John Schlesinger's
Sunday Bloody Sunday. When Kenneth Tynan was prevented from
continuing his theatre column in 1973 because of his job as
dramaturge at the National Theatre, he switched for a while to the
paper's film column, a job for which he was well qualified as a
former film adviser to Ealing (he co-scripted Seth Holt's directorial
debut Nowhere to Go) and the future producer of Polanski's
MacBeth. Another Penelope – Penelope Mortimer – became *The
Observer's* film critic in 1967 and she brought with her the
experience of working with Otto Preminger (she and her then-
husband John scripted Bunny Lake is Missing) and having her
novel The Pumpkin Eater adapted by Harold Pinter for Jack
Clayton to direct. She was succeeded in 1971 by the jazz singer and
writer George Melly, who had written the screenplays for Desmond
Davis's Smashing Time and Jonathan Miller's Take a Girl Like
You. Three years later another writer and jazz musician, Russell

Davies, took over and he wrote the column until the British joint-editor of this dossier became *The Observer's* film critic in 1978.

The dossier is a collection of new material and previously published pieces that have not been readily available in this country. As co-editors we have written essays drawing on our experience of journalism and the cinema on different sides of the Atlantic. The cultural historians Jeffrey Richards and Michel Cieutat, both of whom make film central to their teaching and interpretation of 20th Century history, have contributed original articles on newspaper movies in Britain and on the Continent. In addition we have included important, not easily accessible pieces by Samuel Fuller and Loren Ghiglione. Fuller's piece was originally commissioned by the American co-editor of this dossier for a newspaper season mounted at the Museum of Fine Arts, Boston, in 1974. Ghiglione, a past president of the American Society of Newpaper Editors and a working journalist (as Editor of *The News* in Southbridge, Massachusetts), allowed republication of a chapter of the catalogue which accompanies his Library of Congress exhibition on the journalist and popular culture currently on a multi-year tour of sites in the United States, The American Journalist: Paradox of the Press.
Additional material is included on press films from American movie books not published in Great Britain, and we also present a selected filmography, made by the editors and Karl French, with the usual acknowledgements to *Variety*, *The Monthly Film Bulletin*, Dennis Gifford's *British Film Catalogue* and the *American Film Institute Catalogue of Motion Pictures*.

Both this Dossier and the seasons at the NFT are a labour of love, which come from our lifelong fascination and professional involvement with movies and newspapers. Between them, they shaped the culture of our century, merging in recent years into the hybrid forms of television. This dossier looks back to some of the sources of the way we came to perceive the world: the book is probably best read while dressed in shirt-sleeves and wearing a green visor.

P.F / D.R   July 1991.

CONTENTS

FROM CLASSROOM TO NEWSROOM

PHILIP FRENCH

Like many people of my working-class/lower-middle-class back-ground born in Britain between the wars, I grew up in thrall to American movies. In them I found what we now call my role models. The earliest figure to attract me was, of course, the cowboy. But although I continued to like the Western above all other genres, it gradually became clear that a life on the range was mere fantasy. It would not only entail learning to ride and shoot, I would also have to move back to the nineteenth century. As a serious vocational guide the cowboy was replaced by the cop, the private eye and the newspaperman, and after seriously toying for a while with the idea of joining the police force (my closest friend in Liverpool did go on to the Merseyside police academy), my ambitions came to focus on journalism.

What I wanted to be was an American journalist. The occasional British films on the subject did not excite me. Barry K. Barnes, as the dashing Fleet Street ace Simon Drank in This Man is News (1938) and its sequel This Man In Paris, struck me as an uxorious middle-class twit. George Formby as the photographer breaking into Fleet Street in I See Ice (1938) was his usual gormless self, and though we loved George we knew that he was a northern hick being patronised and laughed at by southerners. Moreover the editor George sought to impress was played by the usual authority figure in Formby comedies, the cheerful, bald, moustachioed Garry Marsh, who had a disturbing resemblance to my father and the fathers of most of my friends. Norman Wooland and Sarah Churchill as the investigative reporters exposing minor local government chicanery for their small West Country newspaper in All Over the Town (1948) were an attractive couple – he had played

Horatio to Olivier's Hamlet, she was the real-life daughter of Winston Churchill. But they seemed altogether too English and (which is, I suppose, a compliment to Derek Twist's film) all too like the reality I might have experienced working for a British provincial paper – and the crusading highpoint of that reality! The journalists that most appealed to me were the real-life war correspondents Alan Wood and Stanley Maxted who returned to Holland eighteen months after the actual battle to re-enact their coverage of the Arnhem operation along with men of the British Airborn Forces in Brian Desmond Hurst's documentary reconstruction Theirs is the Glory (1946). I came to know this film well in the 1950s. It was constantly being shown at the Airborne Forces Depot in Aldershot and as a morale boosting re-vaccination exercise when I severed with the Parachute Regiment.

What most of these British feature films lacked was danger, clamour and social status. In the United States and in American movies there was not the same sharp division between the big national papers and the provincial press. The great metropolitan papers of New York, Chicago and San Francisco were featured in The Front Page, Five Star Final and Nothing Sacred. But there were also major newspapers in sizeable cities across the country with local battles to be fought against corrupt politicians and gangsters: typically in Deadline USA (1952), Humphrey Bogart is fighting to preserve his great liberal daily on two fronts – against a powerful mobster in league with local politicians and against slick competitors interested only in turning an easy buck.

Then there were small-town newspapers that conferred upon their editors a social position far superior to that enjoyed by local journalists in Britain. For example, the mature, generous, worldly wise paterfamilias in Eugene O'Neill's delightful, nostalgic comedy of turn-of-the-century New England life, Ah, Wilderness is a small-town New England newspaper editor and MGM did not stint on the casting. In the 1935 film version he was played by Lionel Barrymore. In the 1946 musical re-make, Summer Holiday, the role was taken by Walter Huston. Nat Miller, as this quietly heroic man is called, did not have to leave home to find a satisfying role in life.

On the more colourful, bustling big city scene, the crusading journalist is not intimately involved in a close-knit community, but his challenges are larger, he is less innocent and his responsibilities are in constant need of redefinition. He is an independent hero fighting for truth and justice on the part of society and the man in the street, against local oligarchies and crime syndicates. And he is not sure of victory. His speech and demeanour are not noticeably different from the cynical, opportunistic hack at the next desk or employed by the rival newspaper. Like the Western, one of the attractive aspects of the journalism movie is that you can enjoy the company of both the hero and the villain. In some cases the hero can begin as one and end up as the other. In most of his post-war Westerns James Stewart plays a former outlaw seeking redemption for his depredations or as a self-centered opportunist converted to distinterested moral activity. This particular character, which recurs throughout his Anthony Mann Westerns, was anticipated by Henry Hathaway's great 1948 newspaper movie Call Northside 777, in which Stewart plays a Chicago reporter. He starts out writing about an alleged miscarriage of justice a quarter of a century before during Prohibition, exploiting an immigrant mother's belief in her son's innocence as a human interest story for circulation-building pathos. He ends up risking his career by taking on the police force and the Cook County judicial system to secure the freedom of a wrongly convicted man.

In 1956 in my final year as an undergraduate at Oxford, I applied for an English-Speaking Union Scholarship to study journalism in the United States on the flimsy basis of having edited the university magazine The Isis and written a weekly column for the university newspaper The Cherwell. I was offered a graduate teaching assistantship at Indiana University and I cannot convey the excitement I felt when the formal letter of confirmation came from the Department of Journalism. The notepaper heading announced that the Journalism School was located at Ernie Pyle Hall, named for the great Hoosier journalist who became the most popular frontline reporter of World War II. Pyle died in action in the Pacific in April 1945 and was impersonated the following year by Burgess Meredith in William Wellman's The Story of G.I. Joe (released in

Britain as War Correspondent). While covering the war in Western Europe Ernest Hemingway described himself as "Ernie Haemorrhoid, the poor man's Pyle." When I got to Indiana I found that the main auditorium in Ernie Pyle Hall was named for another Indiana graduate who had been killed in the line of duty – the editor of a small-town newspaper in neighbouring Ohio, murdered by the gangsters whose activities he'd been exposing.

My year in Bloomington, the main campus of Indiana University, was a sobering rather than a disillusioning experience. My romantic, idealistic vision of journalism was shared by relatively few people at Ernie Pyle Hall, whether they belonged to the highly experienced faculty (the department was headed by a former city editor of the New York *World Telegram and Sun*, feature writing was taught by a onetime editor of *Reader's Digest*, then under contract to *The Saturday Evening Post*), the small body of graduate students (all bent on teaching high-school journalism or joining the business side of newspapers), or the students taking their AB degrees with a major or minor in journalism. The last were a mixed bunch, the vast majority of whom set their sights no higher than small-town dailies, weeklies or bi-weeklies, with a few high-fliers seeing their future in middle-western metropolitan dailies, magazines or in public relations.

Indiana is the crossroads of America and a great newspaper state, having produced some of the country's finest, and worst, editors and reporters. But in 1957 it hadn't come too well out of the McCarthy era. The state's Senators had supported Joe McCarthy, as had most of the Representatives, and the University daily newspaper had refused satirical advertising from the locally instituted Green Feather Organization, set up as a comic protest against and entirely serious attack on the TV series Robin Hood as a subversive left-wing programme. The advertisements were considered too political. But when I wrote a mildly tendentious weekly column for the student daily and the Dean to Foreign Students attempted to kill it (on the grounds that I was a crypto-Communist sent from Europe to undermine the international goodwill to which he had dedicated his life), the Chairman of the

Journalism Department defended me. He agreed with little that I wrote, but he stood up for the right to freedom of speech and the freedom of the press as constitutionally protected by the First Amendment.

I returned to England in 1958. A condition of ESU awards and the accompanying Fulbright Travel Grants was that after completing full-time study you went back to your country of origin for two and a half years to spread the good word before seeking permanent residence in the United States. A week after getting home, I was told by the kindly editor of *The Daily Herald* (the leading popular left-wing serious daily that metamorphosed into the present *Sun*) that he didn't think I was a 'foot- in-the-door-man'. I belonged, he suggested, to the quality press.

So I joined the *Bristol Evening Post*, the largest circulation daily newspaper in the West of England, as reporter, leader-writer, male fashion correspondent and humorous columnist. I worked there for five months. From time to time I found myself on the same assignments as Tom Stoppard, a general reporter for *The Bristol Evening World*, supposedly a rival journal, but in fact covertly owned by the *Post*. Tom subsequently wrote a couple of splendid plays (The Real Inspector Hound and Night and Day) and an outstanding TV film (Professional Foul) about journalism and journalists.

In 1959, I was appointed second-in-command of the *Evening Post* two-man branch office in Weston-Super-Mare, covering the local magistrates court and attempting to whip up interesting stories in a minor seaside resort out-of-season. I was unaware that John Cleese was living there at the time, eager to leave for Cambridge and theatrical fame. When an offer came to become a producer for BBC Radio I immediately accepted and worked in broadcasting for the next thirty-two years, practicing as a critic and feature writer on the side. As a result my romantic ideas about the press that the classic Hollywood cinema had created were never directly challenged. Some part of my psyche continued and continues to be engaged with these fantasies.

In 1978 my senior colleagues at the BBC suggested that I should revisit Indiana and gather material for a programme reflecting on the changes in American life between my first sojourn in the States and the present. Entering Ernie Pyle Hall after an absence of 20 years, I discovered an eerie silence – word-processors had recently been installed and everyone was poring over their green screens. But when I came to talk to the students, I discovered that while the university, like other campuses, was adjusting to the post-1960s conservative ethos, the Journalism School was full of idealistic fervour. What had inspired this mood was the Watergate scandal, the activities of Woodward and Bernstein, and Alan J. Pakula's film All the President's Men. A couple of years earlier, so the head of Radio-TV told me, the brightest students were all being attracted to his section of the department. They now all wanted to be investigative reporters on newspapers, old-fashioned print journalists. I'm not sure how long this lasted.

Very shortly after there was a reaction against investigative journalism in the cinema and in right-wing journals. Neo-conservative writers began to question the role of civic-minded whistle-blowers and what they considered the presumptuousness of the adversary liberal press. The assumptions behind liberal movies like The Parallax View (1974), Three Days of the Condor (1975) and All the President's Men (1976) were challenged, most significantly by Absence of Malice (1981). Scripted by the Pulitzer Prize-winning journalist Kurt Luedtke, directed by Sydney Pollack, who made Three Days of the Condor, this political thriller appears to be a critique of the excesses of investigative reporting. It is in effect an early Reagan era demolition job, suggesting that the vogue for investigative reporting is the current face of old style yellow journlaism. The populist Sydney Pollack made The Way We Were (1973), in which Barbra Streisand went from the 1930s to the 1960s as an unreconstructed Stalinist, and the Capra-esque fable The Electric Horseman where the roles of innnocent all-American niceguy and tough female reporter that would have been played in the 1930s by Gary Cooper and Jean Arthur were taken in 1979 by Robert Redford and Jane Fonda. In Absence of Malice, a trendy Southern liberal reporter (Sally Field), pointedly named

Megan Carter, is used by an anti-crime task force to plant a newspaper story that Florida liquor merchant Paul Newman, son of a long-dead gang boss, is the chief suspect in the murder of an hispanic union leader. The object is to compel him to finger the real killer, but the result is to damage his business and drive a friend to suicide. He has no legal redress and is forced to devise a fiendish scheme to get his own back. The movie is not just an attack on investigative reporters, it also lashes out at liberated women, the abortion lobby, Cuban dockworkers and over-zealous federal investigators. It was the popular spearhead of a neo-conservative attack on the press and news media in America that has continued from the late 1970s right up to bitter attacks on the coverage of the Gulf War (*Commentary*, May, 1991: "The End of the Vietnam Paradigm?" by Joshua Muravchik; "TV News and the Neutrality Principle" by John Corry) and been paralleled in Britain in, for instance, the assaults made on critics of the Falklands War in the early 1980s, the unremitting criticism of the liberal press in Paul Johnson's weekly media column in *The Spectator*, and the concerted attacks made by right-wing newspapers on the TV programme Death on the Rock (about the SAS killing of IRA terrorists in Gibralter) and the journalists who sought, successfully in the event, to re-open the cases of the innocent men and women given long sentences for their alleged roles in the Guildford and Birmingham IRA pub bombings.

Thinking about my visit to the newsroom of the Indiana *Daily Student* at Ernie Pyle Hall in 1978, I'm sure that the silence was the most memorable feature. It was my first experience of the new technology and I now appreciate that noise and bustle are central to the newspaper movie: the clatter of typewriters in the newsroom, the ringing of phones, the raising of voices, the thunder of the presses in the basement below. The throbbing of the newspaper was part of the dynamic atmosphere of the city itself. Not surprisingly therefore, one can date the classic period of the newspaper as an informal genre as following shortly after the coming of sound to Hollywood.

There were of course movies set in newspaper offices in the silent era and as Kevin Brownlow has demonstrated in Behind the Mask of Innocence (1991), his study of the social movie in early American cinema, the American filmmakers of the early 20th Century were closely allied to the muck-raking journalists of the Age of Reform. But sadly in 1915 the U.S. Supreme Court ruled that the movies were a business 'pure and simple', not to be protected by the Constitution; the decision was not reversed until 1951. The movie moguls also lured some gifted journalists to California, most notably the former Chicago *Tribune* and New York *Times* writer Herman J. Mankeiwicz and the veteran of several Chicago dailies, Ben Hecht. Mankiewicz, who was to be co-author of the greatest newspaper movie, Citizen Kane, arrived in Hollywood early in 1926. Later that year he invited Ben Hecht, soon to become co-author of the greatest of all newspaper comedies, The Front Page, to join him. His telegram famously read: "Will you accept 300 per week to work for Paramount Pictures? All Expenses paid. Millions are to be grabbed out here and your only competition is idiots. Don't let it get around."

With the coming of sound, word did get around and scores of journalists flocked to a Hollywood in desperate need of people who could produce sharp, punchy dialogue, who could work to deadlines without putting on literary airs, and who knew their way around town. What they knew best was newspapers and they wrote scripts for hundreds of movies aggrandising, excoriating or merely exploiting (for laughs and thrills) their old profession. In the process they turned journalists and their female counterparts, the sob sisters, into popular heroes and heroines, and often anti-heroes and heroines, on a part with cowboys, cops, gangsters, private eyes, aviators, explorers, hoofers and other favourites of the silver screen. Few of them returned to their ill-paid trade, though one long-forgotten actress went the other way – the B-feature star Elaine Shepard (her movies included I Cover Chinatown, a 1937 comedy about tour-guides not journalists) quit Hollywood to become a reporter and even wrote an autobiography with the catchy title Forgive Us Our Press Passes.

The golden Age of the Hollywood newpaper film was from the early 1930s to America's entry into World War II, from the first version of The Front Page (1931), a raucous celebration of cut-throat yellow journalism, to Citizen Kane, a complex examination of how a great newspaper proprietor came to betray his early ideals. Not every Hollywood star appeared in Westerns or musicals, but at some time or another every star played a journalist. One recalls Edward G. Robinson as the conscientious editor being forced down-market by his venal proprietors in Five Star Final (1931); Fredric March as the journalist exploiting the supposed imminent death of Carole Lombard in Nothing Sacred (1937), the most savage of all satires on unscrupulous newspapermen; James Cagney as the crusading reporter framed by the mob in Each Dawn I Die (1939); James Stewart as the left-wing reporter reluctantly covering a society wedding in The Philadelphia Story (1940); Spencer Tracy and Katharine Hepburn working together for the first time as a tough sports reporter married to a sophisticated political columnist in Woman of the Year (1942), a film they immediately followed up with Keeper of the Flame, in which a reporter (Tracy) finds out that the widow (Hepburn) of a recently deceased national celebrity has discovered that her late husband was a fascist plotting to overthrow the U.S. government.

Many character actors specialised in newspaper roles, mixing them with parts as gangsters, convicts and backstage staff – as a tribute to this familiar bunch Billy Wilder gave a small role in his version of The Front Page to the septuagenarian Allen Jenkins, who died before the film opened. Lee Tracy, who created the role of Hildy Johnson in the 1928 Broadway production of The Front Page was brought out to Hollywood and type-cast for the next dozen years as a fast-talking reporter in low-budget movies with titles like Clear All Wires, Behind the Headlines, and Power of the Press. In one of his few pre-war appearances out of the B-Western saddle, John Wayne appeared in I Cover the War (1937) as a newsreel cameraman reporting from the Spanish Civil War. Fortunately for the Duke's subsequent reputation, the character he played is re-assigned to a minor colonial war in Africa before he could be contaminated by Spanish Republican propaganda.

The stereotypes of the tough editor chomping a cigar, the brash crime reporter demanding that the city desk 'hold the front page' and the suave foreign correspondent scooping his rivals and swapping racy banter with female competitors in distant hot spots shaped the public attitude towards the press and influenced the way newspaper people thought of themselves. But the filmmakers were really helping to consolidate the legendary, romantic role that journalists had played in American life since pre-Revolutionary days when editors had led the oppostition to George III's rule (Benjamin Franklin was himself a printer, newspaper publisher and phamphleteer) and the Founding Fathers enshrined the Freedom of the Press in the First Amendment to the Constitution. Traditionally in any frontier town the first institutions set up after the blacksmith's forge and the saloon were the church, the schoolroom and the newspaper office. The printer-cum-newspaper-owner is an important figure in the Western (all pictures about the gunfight at the OK Corral feature Tombstone's paper *The Epitaph*) and in Kirk Douglas's Watergate Western Posse (1975), an idealistic crippled editor bent on exposing a corrupt frontier politician combines the function of the Woodward-Bernstein team and the impaired Vietnam veteran. Perhaps the most memorable Western newspaper office is the one in the frontier community of Shinbone in John Ford's The Man Who Shot Liberty Valance (1962), which produced a line almost as well-known as Bogart's "Play it Sam" and as often misquoted. When asked by politician James Stewart if he's going to publish the true story of Liberty Valance's death, the young reporter Carlton Young says (referring to his paper's former editor Edmond O'Brien): "No, sir. As our late and great editor, Dutton Peabody, used to say: 'It ain't news. This is the West. When the legend becomes a fact, print the legend.'"

The journalist had, and has, a special function as the ideal representative of the filmmaker and the audience. To a much greater extent than those other inquiring figures – the cop, the federal agent, the private eye and the priest – the reporter is licensed to cross social divides, move around the country, go abroad. It is his duty to observe, ask questions, seek out the truth.

At best he is a crusader for justice, a disinterested servant of the public good, combining some of the functions of the priesthood without being clothed in sanctity. He is the guardian of the well of truth; he can also be the polluter of that source. Over the past 60 years the movie journalist has reflected the doubts and confidence of the American public in the democratic process. He is, in the phrase Edmund Wilson coined to describe the public role of Ernest Hemingway, "a gauge of morale."

The movie journalist is, of course, a generalist, covering the domestic, national or international scene. Specialists tend towards eccentricity or extreme individuality, their sexuality often suspect – the drama critic played by Clifton Webb in Laura and George Sanders in All About Eve; the role of the film critic that Woody Allen wrote for himself in Play It Again Sam; or in England, the countryside correspondent John Boot sent by Lord Copper to cover a war in Africa for *The Daily Beast* in Evelyn Waugh's novel Scoop (adapted as a TV film by William Boyd and directed by Gavin Millar in 1988 with Michael Maloney as Boot) and Alec Guinness as the gardening correspondent assigned by his Fleet Street newspaper to take care of some prize-winning Welsh readers visiting London for an international football match in the Ealing comedy A Run For Your Money (1949). In the clever horror movie Theatre of Blood (1973), a bitterly disgruntled classic actor played by Vincent Price wreaks his revenge on the effete members of the London Critics' Circle by killing them one by one in parodic re-creations of bloody scenes from Shakespeare. The cinema's most significant specialist is, unquestionably, Jed Leland (Joseph Cotten), Charles Foster Kane's first appointment (as drama critic) upon becoming proprietor of the New York *Inquirer*; he is at once the dubious keeper of Kane's conscience and the judge of his performance on the public stage. Kane humiliates Leland, but nothing like as thoroughly as James Cagney's treatment of a movie critic in Lady Killer (1933). As a New York hoodlum turned Hollywood star, Cagney escorts the hapless tuxedo-clad scribe from his table at the Cocoanut Grove to the men's lavatory where he forces him literally to eat a column in which he had criticised Cagney and his female co-star.

Like James Stewart in Call Northside 777, the movie reporter invariably becomes the hero of the story he's writing. The most significant exception is Citizen Kane. The almost faceless reporter Thompson, charged by the editors of News On the March (a slightly disguised March of Time) with discovering the identity of 'Rosebud', is a pure catalyst, an agent of change wholly unaffected by the changes he brings about. Inquiring into the life of a man who began his career owning a newspaper called The Inquirer, he is seen from behind, in half-profile or in deep concealing shadows. We learn almost everything about Kane, and nothing about Thompson. His Christian name – Jerry – is provided in the final minute and if we met him in a bar we would not recognise him.

After World War II, as TV came to eclipse the cinema as a medium of entertainment and to challenge print as the principal source of news, the newspaper movie declined as a Hollywood staple. It didn't die, and four major stars had their most memorable newspaper roles in the post-war decade: Gregory Peck as the WASP reporter posing as a Jew to expose anti-semitism in the sombre Gentleman's Agreement (1947) – Peck also had a marvellous part as a foreign correspondent six years later in the light-hearted Roman Holiday; Kirk Douglas as a disgraced big city journalist exploiting a local tragedy in New Mexico to buy his ticket back into the big time in Ace in the Hole (1951); Bogart as already mentioned in the anti-McCarthy vindication of liberal values, Deadline USA (1952); Burt Lancaster as the grotesque right-wing columnist (modelled on Walter Winchell, who played himself in a couple of pre-war newspaper films) speaking poison across America from his Broadway lair in Sweet Smell of Success.

Hollywood never felt threatened by radio. Moviemakers began early on to collaborate with the sound medium. There are numerous films set in radio studios and most are affectionate. The response to TV after World War II (follwing on from some wide-eyed pictures like W.C. Field's 1933 International House and Edward Dmytryk's 1939 Televsiion Spy), was a hostility bred of fear. The cinema treated TV with contempt, mocking those who worked in it and the programmes transmitted. The latter were usually cheap westerns shown out of focus or crass game-shows; a running gag was to show breakdowns in transmission. By the 1970s, however, Tinseltown had had two decades of producing series of TV and making its back list available to the small screen. It was now hooked on the glamour of the not-so-new medium. Peter Bogdanovich's The Last Picture Show, made in 1971 and looking back to Texas in 1951, affectionately brought together the movies of the early 1950s, the TV programmes of the time (most notably Sid Caesar's Show of Shows), and the pop music heard on the air waves. The most acerbic radio film is probably The Great Man (1956), a mini-Citizen Kane, written and directed by José Ferrer. As a radio reporter assigned to make an adulatory obituary of a celebrated broadcaster, Ferrer discovers the man's feet of clay and goes on the air with a demolition job. This glib, slick, attention-grabbing movie anticipates Elia Kazan's A Face in the Crowd (1957), an exposé of a potential TV demagogue. In screenwriter Budd Schulberg's short story "Your Arkansas Traveller", written in the early 1950s, the central character is a folksy, fascistic radio star.

In her 1971 essay "Raising Kane", Pauline Kael saw Citizen Kane as the culmination of the newspaper movies of the 1930s, a sort of combination of the high spirits of The Front Page and the liberal censoriousness of Five Star Final. "It manages," she wrote, "to create something aesthetically exciting and usable out of the playfulness of American muckraking satire." She also noted in its form – the reporter from a newsreel based closely on Henry Luce's The March of Time looking into the career of a newspaper tycoon – the first indication of an historical shift from a culture centering on print to one increasingly concerned with visual images. The progress Kael notes can be seen in the four versions of the Hecht-MacArthur play The Front Page. In 1931 it was a rough, amoral, wise-cracking newspaper comedy. In 1940, under the direction of Howard Hawks it became the sleek, sophisticated His Girl Friday, a variation of the late 1930s screwball comedy that the Harvard philosopher Stanley Cavell dubbed "The Hollywood Comedy of Remarriage" in his book Pursuits of Happiness (1981). The hero Hildy Johnson has been turned into an ace woman correspondent

(Rosalind Russell) and the hard-bitten editor Walter Burns (Cary Grant), who'll stop at nothing to retain the services of his star reporter now becomes Hildy's ex-husband. In the 1974 film, Billy Wilder goes back to the original title, adds some fashionable bad language, lays on the late 1920s nostalgic detail with a trowel, and turns the play into an Odd Couple buddy-buddy movie by casting Jack Lemmon and Walter Matthau in the leading roles. Thirteen years later, in Ted Kotcheff's wretched Switching Channels (1987), His Girl Friday is the source, the setting is a 24-hour cable news station of no clearly discernable standing whose manager (Burt Reynolds) conspires to keep his ex-wife (Kathleen Turner) working for him as the station's top reporter.

In moving from newspapers to TV there is an immense loss of individuality and a considerable gain in visual glamour. A star like Jane Fonda isn't going to languish behind a type-writer or word-processor when she can be out there in the streets emoting, microphone in hand, in The China Syndrome and The Electric Horseman. But as Broadcast News (1987) demonstrates, the TV reporter is just one member of a team involved in a complex technical operation, subservient to the producer and the anchor-man. However dim the latter might be, he dominates the screen because he can pick up cues, wear his clothes well, control his sweat glands and exude the right confident charm.

As Jeffrey Richards and Michel Cieutat agree in their contributions to this dossier on the press movies of Britain and the Continent, European filmmakers are working in the shadow of Hollywood. With monotonous regularity the British B-feature thrillers have starred minor American actors as visiting reporters (usually solving crimes). British filmmakers have usually gone abroad to make real heroes of journalists – to South Africa to record the reisistance to the authorities of Donald Woods, the liberal editor who became a friend of black activist Steve Biko, in Cry Freedom (1987) and the Communist opponent of Apartheid, Ruth First in A World Apart (1988); and to Cambodia to observe the dilemma of New York Times reporter Sydney Schanberg, forced to leave his local assistant to the mercy of the Khmer Rouge in The Killing Fields (1984).

Woods, First and Schanberg were all played by Americans, though marginal roles were found for British actors – in The Killing Fields, for instance, Julian Sands impersonated the *Sunday Times* reporter John Swain. Curiously one of the many disastrous changes wrought by Hollywood in bringing Tom Wolfe's The Bonfire of the Vanities to the screen was to turn one of the novel's chief villains, Peter Fallow, the seedy drunken British journalist working for the New York tabloid *The City of Light*, into an American.

As a film critic for *The Spectator* in the 1930s, Graham Greene compared British newspaper movies adversely with their American counterparts and as a novelist he created three fictional journalists of unforgettable seediness. The first is Minty, the expatriate freelance hack in England Made Me, impersonated in the 1972 film by Michael Hordern. The second is Hale, the sweaty Fleet Street crime reporter in Brighton Rock (played in the 1948 film by Alan Sheatley) who exposed the Sussex racecourse gangs and has been sent back to Brighton on a demeaning circulation-building assignment (a function inspired by the *News-Chronicle's* perennial Lobby Ludd campaign). It leads inevitably to his murder, the dramatic trigger of Greene's entertainment. The third and most significant is Fowler, the embittered foreign correspondent covering the last days of France's Indo-China War in The Quiet American, published in 1955, less than 18 months after the fall of Dien Biene Phu, and controversially filmed by Joseph L. Mankiewicz in 1958 starring Michael Redgrave. The movie turned the novel's critique of American foreign policy on its head, thus robbing its self-despising hero of his one, supremely redeeming feature – his political sagacity.

But ten years later, as Michael Herr noted in his Vietnam chronicle Despatches (1977), the film of The Quiet American was forgotten and Greene's novel was in the knapsack of every correspondent covering the Vietnam War. There is an interesting comparison to be made between Fowler, the disgusted, detatched correspondent with a liking for the odd pipe of opium, and the unnamed photojournlist played by Dennis Hopper, a character inspired by Sean Flynn and high on less soothing drugs, in Apocalypse Now, for which Herr wrote the hero's voice-over commentary. The transition isn't merely from typewriter to camera, from words to image. We can see here a major transformation of sensibility, a mutation of morality, a movement from criticism via commitment to complicity. This ethical spectrum is examined in a number of movies about the foreign correspondent, whose role has become infinitely more complex in the 50 years since Joel McCrea, as Hitchcock's American innocent Foreign Correspondent in Europe at the outbreak of World War II, had his work cut out distinguishing between crypto-fascists and pacifists. The most notable are Volker Schlöndorff's politically tendentious Circle of Deceit (1981), the best feature film to come out of reporting the hell of Beirut, and Roger Spottiswoode's Under Fire (1983), a complex movie that moves from a post-colonial war in Africa to the final year of the Somoza regime in Nicaragua as observed by the press, radio, TV and a photo-journalist attempting unsuccessfully to remain a disinterested observer.

Traditionally Americans have seen the cinema as central to life, but not as an art form, and the journalist as a major, heroic figure in the national discourse. Europeans on the other hand have seen the cinema as an art form but not central to life, and the newspaperman as a marginal, somewhat disreputable person. This explains certain differences between representations of the press and journalists in European and U.S. pictures. But it is only the beginning of such an explanation.

THE JOURNALIST IN BRITISH FILMS

JEFFREY RICHARDS

Sherlock Holmes: The journalist in British films is rather like the curious incident of the dog in the night time.
Dr. Watson: But the dog did nothing in the night time, Holmes.
Sherlock Holmes: Nor did the journalist in British films.

The newspaperman has been one of the heroes of American democracy. Among the most enduring images of the United States which has impressed itself upon the global memory is that of the eager, bright-eyed reporter, trenchcoated and trilby-hatted, racing into the noisy, bustling newsroom and shouting 'Hold the Front Page'. The American newspaperman has come to symbolize both for domestic and overseas audiences key elements of the American myth. He is the defender of the Constitution and of the rights of the individual. He is the symbol of freedom of access to information and uses this role to expose corruption, oppression, manipulation and exploitation. He is the embodiment of the crackling pace of U.S. life, that world of wailing sirens, screeching tires, machine gun bullets and special editions. He is populist Urban Man, outwardly tough, shrewd, wisecracking but with a heart of gold, a broad streak of sentimentality, a fund of robust common sense and under a protective veneer of cynicism, a core of essential decency. He has figured in every conceivable Hollywood genre, not just comedy, drama and melodrama, but western, horror film, thriller, sci-fi. What many critics would regard as the greatest ever Hollywood film, Citizen Kane, is an imaginative biopic of newspaper tycoon William Randolph Hearst and uses the newspaper world as a metaphor for American life and history.

The newspaperman has been mythified and apotheosized by being clad in the flesh and features of familiar and well-loved stars, who have lent him some of their own special glamour. Thus the newspaperman as champion of democracy has been represented by Spencer Tracy exposing American fascism in Keeper of the Flame (1943), by James Cagney exposing Japanese fascism in Blood on the Sun (1945), by Robert Redford and Dustin Hoffman uncovering the truth about Watergate in All the President's Men (1976) and Warren Beatty probing the mysterious murder of a JFK-type politico in The Parallax View (1974). The newspaperman as detective has solved crimes: Ben Lyon in I Cover the Waterfront (1933) and James Stewart in Call Northside 777 (1947). The newspaperman as social investigator has exposed prison conditions (James Cagney in Each Dawn I Die), institutional anti-Semitism (Gregory Peck in Gentleman's Agreement) and the state of insane asylums (Peter Breck in Shock Corridor). The newspaperman as war correspondent has chronicled the battlefield experiences of 'our boys': Henry Hull in Objective Burma (1945), Burgess Meredith in The Story of G.I. Joe (1945), and David Janssen in The Green Berets (1968). The newspaperman as the exponent of law and order has resisted the depredations of the bad guys in frontier towns: Edmond O'Brien's Falstaffian Dutton Peabody in The Man Who Shot Liberty Valance (1962) and Randolph Scott's guntoting Ned Britt in Fort Worth (1951), his credo: 'The presses are a thousand times more potent than gunpowder'. Frank Capra's archetypal populist heroes were often newspapermen (Robert Williams in Platinum Blonde, Clark Gable in It Happened One Night, Bing Crosby in Here Comes the Groom). And when his heroes were not, his heroines were: Jean Arthur in Mr. Deeds Goes to Town and Mr. Smith Goes to Washington, Barbara Stanwyck in Meet John Doe. For the newspaperwoman shared the qualities and characteristics of the newspaperman (for example Katharine Hepburn in Woman of the Year and Bette Davis in Front Page Woman) so much so that in his 1940 remake of the classic newspaper play The Front Page, retitled His Girl Friday, Howard Hawks changed the battling, conniving, fast-talking reporters from two men (Adolphe Menjou and Pat O'Brien in the 1931 version) to a man and a woman (Cary Grant and Rosalind Russell) without any damage to the structure and nature of the work. The darker side of the press too has been chronicled, the ruthless, singleminded, 'anything for a headline' attitude so perfectly epitomized by Kirk Douglas in Ace in the Hole (1950). But that is the price that is paid for open government and for every cynical exploiter there are a dozen integrity figures crusading in the best traditions of the fourth estate.

Britain has had a newspaper history every bit as colourful and dramatic as the United States. There is abundant material for drama in the struggles of the radical underground press of the 19th century and the heroic efforts of crusading journalists like William Cobbett, in the launch of the mass circulation Sunday newpapers by proto-tycoons like G.W.M. Reynolds and Edward Lloyd in the mid-19th century, in the appearance of the tabloid and the illustrated press in the later 19th century, in the fierce circulation wars of the 1920s and 1930s, in the rise and fall, takeover and merger, launch and relaunch of newspapers, in the Wapping revolution. There have been titanic figures in the history of British journalism, from the legendary editors (like J.T. Delane of *The Times*, J.L. Garvin of *The Observer*, C.P. Scott of *The Manchester Guardian*) to the dashing war correspondents of the 19th century (William Howard Russell, G.W. Steevens and Archibald Forbes), from the fearless social investigators (Henry Mayhew, James Greenwood, W.T. Stead) to the Kane-type proprietors like Lord Northcliffe and Lord Beaverbrook. There has been a whole succession of novelists rooted in the world of journalistic deadlines from Charles Dickens and Rudyard Kipling to Graham Greene and Frederick Forsyth. Yet for all this, no one has produced the great British novel of journalism. Dickens, who provided vivid pictures of the worlds of commerce, the law and the theatre, never gave us his vision of the world of newspapers. Kipling touched on the adventures of the imperial war correspondents in The Light That Failed (filmed by Hollywood in 1939) and Trollope dramatized the role of *The Times* (which he renamed *The Jupiter*) in church politics in the Barsetshire novels. The British cinema, notoriously given to taking its lead from novels and plays, has similarly failed to exploit the dramatic, historical and metaphorical richness of the world of the newspaper.

In British films, real-life war correspondents have made guest appearances in historical films: William Howard Russell as played by Henry Edwards in The Lady With a Lamp (1951) and T.P. McKenna in Charge of the Light Brigade (1967), Charles L. Norris-Newman as played by Ronald Lacey in Zulu Dawn (1979). But they have been very much part of the supporting cast. Winston Churchill's spell as a newspaperman was duly covered in Young Winston (1972) with Simon Ward. But there has been no British cinematic equivalent of Arthur Kennedy's Jackson Bentley in Lawrence of Arabia (1962), a pseudonymous version of American newsman Lowell Thomas who helped to create the legend of Lawrence in the world media, or of Joel McCrea's Huntley Haverstock broadcasting to America from the heart of Blitzed London in Hitchcock's Foreign Correspondent (1940), a fictional character but one whose actions and message were paralleled in real life by CBS's Edward R. Murrow.

There has been no British biopic of Northcliffe or Beaverbrook, no "Lord Kane" to chronicle the genius and the follies of the tycoons who shaped the fortunes of the industry over the past century. Where they have appeared, British newspaper proprietors have been cast in the mould of booming teddy bear like Robert Morley's Lord Rawnsley, launching the London to Paris air race in Those Magnificent Men in Their Flying Machines (1964), or beneficent deus ex machina like Eric Berry's Lord Otterbourne (popularly known as 'The Otter') in the Group 3 comedy Miss Robin Hood (1953).

There has been almost no attempt to create a native cinematic newspaper idiom. One of the very few films to try was John Baxter's Doss House (1933), which, made for £4,000 virtually on a single set, charted a night spent in a Bloomsbury doss house by a disguised reporter looking for an escaped convict. It is a film identical in form and content with James Greenwood's classic of Victorian social exploration, A Night in a Workhouse (1866).

But for the most part British film-makers have sought to imitate proven American models. In some cases they have produced capable and entertaining imitations. In 1936 Brian Desmond Hurst directed a screen version of the stage play The Murder Gang by George Munro and Basil Dean. It was punchily retitled Sensation! (complete with exclamation mark). The 'Murder Gang' of the title are the crowd of crime reporters who descend on the scene of every major criminal slaying and then seek to upstage each other in getting the details. In this case a local waitress and village beauty is murdered. The film is part whodunnit (though seasoned thriller watchers will guess the identity of the murderer early on) and part exposé of journalistic dirty tricks. It is the latter aspect that is the most interesting, as the film follows the activities of ruthless *Daily Post* crime reporter Pat Heaton, who tricks and harasses a suspect's wife and craftily obtains her love letters for publication in his paper. But this is counterbalanced by the fact that he correctly identifies and traps the murderer. Fastmoving and fast-talking in the approved American 30s manner, the film intercuts the methodical police investigations with the unorthodox activities of the journalists, drinking, sleuthing, dictating their stories over the telephone and prepared to do almost anything to 'get a story'. The casting of the habitually grim-visaged and unsmiling American actor John Lodge as Pat Heaton gives the reporter's activities a more uncomfortable reality and the film a sharper critical edge than a more charming or bland British actor would have done. So this tightly shot and unpretentious little film emerges as something of an English version of that unsparing Hollywood exposé of the ethics of the yellow press, Five Star Final (1931).

The model for David MacDonald's This Man Is News (1938) is MGM's Thin Man series of comedy thrillers. Barry K. Barnes and Valerie Hobson play *Gazette* reporter Simon Drake and his wife Pat, a wisecracking, hard-drinking, affectionate team whose inspiration is clearly William Powell and Myrna Loy's Nick and Nora Charles. Alastair Sim, an everpresent in 1930s British films, contributes a characteristic cameo as the excitable Gazette editor MacGregor. Simon Drake, getting too close to the identity of the Ritz-Plaza jewel robbery gang, is the target of several murder attempts. These, his investigations and running battles at the newspaper office make up the action of a lively and watchable film which almost matches its Hollywood inspiration for pace, polish and wit. Its success inspired a sequel, This Man In Paris (1939), in which Drake unmasked a banknote forger, before the war overtook the cinema and the mood and nature of British films underwent a seachange.

The new seriousness that characterized British wartime films bore journalistic fruit in Thunder Rock, the 1942 Boulting Brothers film of Robert Ardrey's allegorical play. It centres on the dilemma of English journalist David Charleston (Michael Redgrave) who has retired from the fray to keep a lighthouse in Canada. He is talked back into commitment and rejoining the battle against Fascism by his dialogues with the ghosts of 19th century emigrants from the Old World, seeking a new life in the Americas: in particular a victim of capitalist industrial exploitaiton, a fighter for women's rights and a medical researcher persecuted by ignorance and supersitition. Of particular interest is the flashback sequence which covers Charleston's career as a reporter in the 1930s. He is seen observing and reporting on the growth of Fascism, seeking to alert the world to the dangers of tyranny in a series of hardhitting books but finding his coverage censored and restricted by his editor and the directors of his paper. Although it is called The Daily Argus, the newspaper is clearly meant to represent The Times, a resemblance made more pointed by the fact that the Argus editor, played by Miles Malleson, is made up to resemble The Times's appeasing editor of the 1930s, Geoffrey Dawson.

But after the war, it is back to American models. Derek Twist's All Over the Town (1949), based on R. F. Delterfield's play, has Norman Wooland as an ex-soldier returning to his home town to take over the local newspaper and expose corrupt local businessmen, and Edward Dmytryk's So Well Remembered (1947), based on James Hilton's novel, features John Mills as a crusading local editor fighting social injustice in a Lancashire town. In so doing both are following in the American footsteps of James Cagney in Johnny Come Lately (1943).

Arguably the best British newspaper film is Gordon Parry's Front

Page Story (1953), a vigorous drama, crisply and often wittily written (Jay Lewis and Jack Howells, from a novel by Robert Gaines). It follows a day in the life of John Grant, harassed, hardworking news editor of *The Daily World* as he seeks the headline for tomorrow's edition. He has to handle a dilettante editor and messages from the unseen proprietor 'His Lordship'. The narrative interweaves the pursuit of a scientist handing over atomic secrets to the enemy, a woman on trial for a mercy killing and the archetypal human interest story of the eviction of a group of East End kids. It also takes in the strains on his marriage caused by the pressures of Grant's job. A carefully chosen array of journalistic 'types' people the offices of *The World* - the wise old stager (Joseph Tomelty) who has seen it all; the drunk rehabilitating himself (Walter Fitzgerald); the 'bleeding heart' idealist forever taking up causes (Michael Goodliffe); the cynical and self-interested careerist (Derek Farr). But they all revolve around the strong central figure of Grant, played by Jack Hawkins, whose rugged integrity is put to excellent use and who makes a blazing defence of the journalistic profession when the idealist denounces the newspaper for hounding the mercy-killer to her death after she is run over fleeing from journalists.

Front Page Story successfully captured something of the urgency, energy and nervosity of the old-style newspaper office where the inexorably looming deadline approaches amid the clatter of typewriters, the circulation of copy, the restless coming and going of employees, visitors and informants, and the stimulating lubricant of non-stop coffee and cigarettes. The same 'feel' pervades Val Guest's The Day the Earth Caught Fire (1961). Guest, who had a background in journalism himself, wrote and directed in the 1960s a series of contemporary location-shot thrillers. The Day the Earth Caught Fire was a robust and enthusiastic sci-fi thriller tracing the effects of American and Russian nuclear tests on the earth's orbit, causing it to head directly for the sun. The film intercut the effects of this catastrophe on the earth's atmosphere with the coverage of it by *The Daily Express*. The leading figures were the stock investigative journalist (Edward Judd) with a conscience, a drink problem and an estranged wife, and the science corresponodent

(Leo McKern) seeking to explain and interpret the disaster to an uncomprehending public. The newspaper background was convincing and was given added authenticity by the casting of the legendary *Express* editor Arthur Christiansen as the fictional editor Jefferson. The film ends with four superbombs being detonated in order to alter the earth's orbit yet again, with the *Express* setting two front pages 'World Saved' and 'World Doomed' and everyone sitting down to await the outcome of the experiment. It nicely encapsulates the continuing journalistic imperitives of urgency, topicality and sensationalism. Christiansen played another editor, Gracey of the fictional *Evening Chronicle*, in Guest's later film, 80,000 Suspects (1963), in which the impending disaster was a smallpox epidemic.

The 1980s has seen the rise of the paranoid thriller both in Britain and America, predicated on the notion of the secret state that is out of control. David Drury's Defence of the Realm (1985) was a fine example of this genre, an evocation of a nightmare world in which cars are followed, homes searched, phone calls tapped and rooms bugged as the unseen agents of the faceless system seek to cover up a nuclear near-miss. The staff of *The Daily Despatch* are in this instance democracy's watchdogs with Gabriel Byrne as the young, ambitious, go-getting professional and Denholm Elliot as the canny old boozer with a nose for the truth.

For all the handful of memorable newspaper plays (David Hare and Howard Brenton's Pravda, 1985; Michael Frayn's Alphabetical Order, 1975; Arnold Wesker's The Journalists, 1975), for all the comic felicities of Evelyn Waugh's Scoop and for all the workman-like virtues of the few British newspaper films, it remains the case that the journalist has never occupied the same place in British culture as the newspaperman has in American culture. Why?

Firstly, secrecy and deference rather than investigation and exposé have been the chief characteristics of British society as epitomized by the fact that the rest of the world knew about Edward VIII and Mrs. Simpson long before Britain did because the newspapers deliberately suppressed the facts. The Mass circulation press, with its titled proprietors, has seen its role as consensual, conservative, supportive of the status quo and not on the whole as agents of change.

Secondly, there is – as always – the class system. Until the 1960s the British hero was traditionally a gentleman and journalism has never been a job for a gentleman. Journalists have always been seen as deraciné, liminal figures. The world of Victorian journalism that produced both Mayhew and Dickens was a raffish, prolific, penurious world, in which articles, essays, stories an novels cascaded indiscriminately from the pens of a tribe of clannish, improvident, imaginative Bohemians, fuelled by drink and tobacco. Perhaps the most extreme example of this lifestyle persisting unchanged into the late 20th century is Jeffrey Bernard, so magnificently portrayed by Peter O'Toole in Keith Waterhouse's play Jeffrey Bernard is Unwell. This articulate, ailing, ex-alumnus of Pangbourne Naval College has taken this style to its logical extreme by actually moving into his spiritual home – the Coach and Horses Public House in Soho – and by turning his own daily life into the copy for his weekly *Spectator* column.

Thirdly – and linked to the class system – is the prevalence of the British ethos of amateurism. The journalist, with his scoops, exclusives, word limits, deadlines, is the essential professional, the antithesis of the gentleman amateur. The British cinema, perfectly capable of producing a plethora of stylish gentlemen, was never in its heyday able to produce the equivalent of the tough, twofisted professional, flying by the seat of his pants, living by his wits, always on the edge: the air mail pilot, gold prospector, oil man, racing driver, deep sea fisherman, forest ranger or newspaperman. So where 1930s Hollywood produced not only a whole breed of actors capable of convincingly portraying such professionals, it actually produced actors who seem in retrospect to have spent almost the whole decade playing just journalists, actors like Lee Tracy, Lloyd Nolan, Pat O'Brien and Roscoe Karns.

If there are any genuine native British journalistic archetypes as distinct from American imitations, then they derive from the cultural assumptions listed above. One would be the innocent, ineffectual, unworldly amateur, who strays by accident into the hardhitting world of journalism: Alec Guinness as the gardening correspondent of the Echo, reluctantly put in charge of two roaring boyos from the Valleys up for the cup in A Run For Your Money. 'How much I prefer vegetables to human beings', his plaintive cry would have found an echo in the heart of that other innocent abroad, William Boot, the countryside correspondent accidentally despatched by *The Daily Beast* to cover an African civil war. Although never filmed, *Scoop* has twice been adapted (unsatisfactorily) for television.

The other and perhaps most enduring image of the British journalist is of the seedy drunken hack, downatheel, improvident, cynical, out with a nose for the truth, an eye for a story and the ability, drink or no drink, to meet a deadline. Michael Hordern's Minty in England Made Me (1972), generally regarded as one of the more successful adaptations of Graham Greene, and Denholm Elliot's Vernon Bayliss in Defence of the Realm stand as their permanent celluloid incarnations.

THE JOURNALIST IN EUROPEAN FILMS
or
THE CAPTIVE OF THE LIE

MICHEL CIEUTAT

While the American cinema has turned films about newspapers into a proper sub-genre, from Lewis Milestone's Front Page (1931) to James L. Brooks's Broadcast News (1987), European films (we are not considering British films here) have only treated journalism in a sporadic fashion. It can be background material for a romantic story, as in Vivre pour vivre by Claude Lelouch (1967) or L'homme fragile by Claire Clouzot (1981), or the backdrop to a comedy as in Le Jouet by Francis Veber (1976), or even an abstract reflection on the wish to change his identity which is experienced by the character Jack Nicholson plays in Professione: Reporter (aka: The Passenger) by Michaelangelo Antonioni (1975). There are obviously enough films dealing with the inherent characteristic of journalists to make a viable study of them, but one doesn't find anywhere in the 'Old World' an involvement with this subject comparable to that in the States.

There is undoubtedly a reason for this. The press in France, Italy or Germany is seen very differently from that in America. A true defender of the freedom of thought, protected by the First Amendment, often called the 'Fourth Estate', the American press has frequently found itself put on a pedestal of self-worship by Hollywood filmmakers like Samuel Fuller (Park Row, 1952) and Alan Pakula (All the President's Men, 1976), while its shortcomings have not been ignored (Citizen Kane, Orson Welles, 1941; Absence of Malice, Sydney Pollack, 1981).

In Europe, on the other hand, journalists are usually seen as part of a business operation greedy for spectacular news stories, without any scruples as regards the methods used to obtain them, and being rather more intent on personal success than on a rigorous pursuit of the truth (Vie Privée, Louis Malle, 1962). Furthermore, this generally negative image has stopped the European filmgoer from an easy identification with a representative of a profession which has anyway always seemed to him to be reserved for a privileged and somewhat dishonest person (cf. the very 'positive' way in which Jean Renoir, at the time of the rise of the Popular Front in France, eliminates Batala-Jules Berry via René Lefèvre in Le Crime de Monsieur Lange in 1935). So European journalists were bound to get a bad press in the cinema!

Alienated from Power
Like the politicians seen in the cinema, the journalist is above all a man devoured by ambition. Thus Daniel Gélin, in his explicitly named film Les Dents longues (1953), plays a young reporter bent on quick success. He learns fast from his boss (Louis Seigner) that being smooth and without scruples is what counts. Moving from Canut to Lyon's Progrès, he comes to Paris – France, where he becomes the right-hand man of Jean Chevrier, the typical journalist of the French cinema of the time, a brutal, amoral, but nevertheless likeable adventurer. Soon afterwards he is contacted by a member of the Assemblée Nationale who wants to turn the paper into a political daily. At the risk of losing the woman he loves, the cub reporter throws himself into this project and manages to preserve his integrity as well as his marriage. This movie, unique in Gélin's career, is the archetypal European film about the press.

Here we have: the young journalist hungry for individual success who will turn up again in 1979 in L'Oeil du Maître by Stéphane Kurc; the cynical exploitation of Paul Batala by Renoir's Monsieur Lange which will reappear in Deux Hommes à Manhattan by Jean-Pierre Melville (cf. the role of Pierre Grasset) in 1958, as well as in Fellini's La Dolce Vita (the role played by Mastroianni) in 1959, and in Sbatti il mostro in prima pagina by Marco Bellochio (Bizzanti played by Gian Maria Volonte); the hypocrite ready for any sort of treachery to achieve his goal, who will be haunting certain scenes in Tout le monde il est beau, tout le monde il est gentil by Jean Yanne (1972) as well as Un linceul n'a pas de poches by Jean-Pierre Mocky (1975); and finally the political fixer whom Bellochio will turn into the leading character of his vengeful Sbatti, quite simply a manipulator of opinions, an egotist who, if he were seized by megalomania, would change it into L'Armaguedon (Alain Jessua, 1977) of tomorrow.

Committed to sensationalism

Like William Randolph Hearst, the journalist in the European films continually writes news of little value where the sensational element looks like basic information. Such is the case with Mastroianni's gossip columnist in La Dolce Vita; the 'cowboys' (Philippe Noiret and Pierre Richard) in Un nuage entre les dents by Marco Pico, one of them a specialist on the typewriter, the other with the camera; the varied and bloody miscellany of Dieter Laser, digger-up of political pseudo-scandals which could create out of The Lost Honour of Katarina Blum (Die Verlorene Ehre der Katarina Blum, Volker Schlöndorff, 1975) some happiness for certain right-wing papers in the old German Federal Republic; Gian Maria Volonte, editor-in-chief for whom the Viol (of a young upper-class girl) on the first page is the ideal opportunity for denouncing Italian left-wing politics; Harry Dean Stanton and Harvey Keitel, who in order to get the maximum viewing figures at any price, want to film La Mort en direct (Deathwatch, Bertrand Tavernier, 1980). All of them are Forger(s) as Nicholas Born said, falsifying the 'ordinary absurd' as Günter Grass added on the publication of this novel (Die Falschung) which denounced, according to him, "the commerce in horror. The madness that reasons." All of them, like the character of Georg Laschen played by Bruno Ganz in Volker Schlöndorff's 1981 adaptation of Die Falschung (Circle of Deceit), seem to be nothing but swashbuckling bruisers in the field of lies.

They come over as swashbuckling bruisers in their physical appeal (Jerzy Skolimowski, the photographer in Circle of Deceit), their varied and incessant activities (Yves Montand in Vivre pour vivre), their dynamic working methods (Krystyna Janda in Man of Marble by Andrzej Wajda, 1977), their particularly rebellious spirit (Simone Signoret throughout, and especially at the end of Judith Therpauve by Patrice Chéreau, 1978), even if they are sometimes revealed to be not quite as tough as they seem, like Jean-Claude Bouillon in Philippe Labro's Tout peut arriver (1969), whose professional determination is shaken by his emotional doubts.

But they cease to be bruisers when they gradually discover the vanity of all worldly pursuits as in the finale of La Dolce Vita, or when fate no longer smiles upon them. They then sink into alcoholism like Pierre Grasset in Deux Hommes à Manhattan; into some form of mental derangement like Philippe Noiret and Pierre Richard in Un nuage entre les dents, whose world view is corrupted by their work; into forced infantilism like this same Pierre Richard who is obliged to be *Le Jouet* ('The Toy') of his employer's son; or, even worse, into death as in the case of Jean-Pierre Mocky's Michel Dolannes in Un linceul n'a pas de poches, Antonioni's Jack Nicholson in Passenger, or Wajda's Zbigniew Zapasiewicz in Rough Treatment (1979). The journalist then becomes a man like the others, lured into and trapped within a hall of mirrors.

A Discontented Idealist

The natural victim of his tendency towards sensationalism and the source of a great part of Western brutalisation, (cf. La Grande Lessive about television by Jean-Pierre Mocky, 1968), the European journalist nevertheless knows how to make amends. Like Harvey Keitel in La Mort en direct, he can from time to time present himself like his American counterpart, as an idealist in the service of truth and freedom. In the same way Patrick Chesnais, in Stephane Kurc's L'oeil du maître, works hard to reveal, impose and finally re-establish honest news at the core of a new TV network that has lost its political and social nerve. Similarly Simone Signoret as Chereau's eponymous Judith Therpauve fights against media sharks simply for the right of a small provincial newspaper, *La Libre République*, to exist. But above all there is the truth about public affairs which he insists upon making public in the face of constant opposition from the reactionary forces in Europe of the

60-s and 70s: in Greece (Jacques Perrin in Costa-Gavras' Z), in Italy (Luigi Squarzine in Francesco Rosi's Il Caso Mattei, 1972), in France (Jean-Louis Trintignant in Yves Boisset's L'Attentat, 1972; Jean-Paul Belmondo in Philippe Labro's L'Heritier, 1972), in Poland (Krystyna Janda in Man of Marble, followed by Marian Opania in Wajda's Man of Iron in 1981), in Germany (Jutta Lampe in Margarethe von Trotta's Die Bleierne Zeit/The German Sisters, 1981). They throw truths of all kinds and from all sides into the face of the world in a splendidly anarchic manner, in order better to condemn the pharisees of modern times in the manner of the very "poujadiste" Frenchman Jean Yanne, in Tout le monde il est beau, tout le monde il est gentil, or Jean-Pierre Mocky in Un linceul d'a pas de poches.

A thirst for truth and freedom frequently forces him to elevate himself, like his American model, to the status of investigator. He becomes a journalistic detective for whom observation and deduction are the two most effective weapons: Deux Hommes à Manhattan; Tout peut arriver; Jean-Luc Bideau in La Salamandre by the Swiss filmmaker Alain Tanner (1971); and the best examples from the years 1958-1981 being L'Héritier, Sbatti il mostro in prima pagina, Il caso Mattei, Man of Marble and Die Bleierne Zeit. However, an investigator on the continent which has produced Cervantes, Kafka, Camus, Simenon and Beckett, as well as Prévert, Carné, Spaak, Duvivier and Polanski, must expect regular cultural confrontations with insuperably powerful public and private institutions. This, in contrast with Bogart in Deadline USA, constantly turns the reporter into the victim of either intolerance, whether by gangsters (like Eddie Constantine at the end of John Berry's Je suis un sentimental in 1955) or political forces – fascist ones for Marcello Mastroianni in Una Giornata particolara (A Special Day) by Ettore Scola in 1977, or Marxist as with Zbigniew Zapasiewica in Rough Treatment; or of organized national hypocricy like Jean-Pierre Mocky in Un linceul n'a pas de poches, his French adaptation of Horace McCoy's novel No Pockets in a Shroud.

The idealistic journalist, like the simple workmen of Carne's Le

Jour se lève and Rossellini's Bicycle Thieves, cannot attain satisfaction in a world where happiness has almost always been synonymous with utopia. This is undoubtedly why François Truffaut thought it a good idea to make his obsessive collector of memories another member of this profession in his admirable and sad La Chambre verte, in which Truffaut himself plays the editor of the obituary column of a provincial newspaper in the 1920s.

Translated by Kersti French

HEADLINES TO HEADSHOTS

SAMUEL FULLER

*The man raped a dog? Get a statement from the
dog and I'll run the story.*

*The Pope on the take? Get a statement from
the Pope and I'll finance the film.*

Weaned on Park Row, teamed with reporter Rhea Gore (John
Huston's mother) on my first double-suicide, I made the eventual
transition from newspaperman to filmmaker as the natural leap
from dummy makeup to facial makeup.

Page One and the Screen are bedmates. Working in the morgue
and shooting a movie trigger constant visions. A headline has the
impact of a headshot, pulp and rawstock fight linage and footage,
a news lead is the opening of a film.

8 point Goudy, Widescreen, pica gauge, movieola-reporter and film
director spill blood on the same emotional battlefield of what is fit
to print and what is fit to film. The *thou cannnot* and *thou must not*
pendulum swings from black-and-white facts to Technicolor
fancies.

The newspaper real and movie imaginary sharing blood-stained
scissors, glue, proofs, cement, splicer, work print give twin birth
to the battle cry of rewrite, remake, retake, redub and matures with
the press and projection machine.

Peddling the *Worcester Telegram, Boston Post, Boston American* in

Worcester was my first contact with newspapers. To New York at 11, peddling papers at 12 at the 125th Street Ferry. In those days newsboys bought papers from the Circulation Department. A love affair started with the *New York Evening Journal*, 238 William Street, off Park Row, a column away from the Bowery, across from the Newsboys' Home sponsored by Al Smith. One-eyed, half-deaf Tom Foley, foreman of the *Journal's* press room, opened up Wonderland, showed me presses in action, Linotypes singing in Composing, and finally gold itself: the City Room on the seventh floor.

The shouts of "Copy, boy!!" with young men in late teens running, making "books", shooting copy thru pneumatic tubes was electrifying. The hell with peddling newspapers. Working on one became an obsession. Working on the *Journal*.

"Lie," Managing Editor Joseph V. Mulcahy said. "Tell 'em your're 14 to get working papers. Then I'll put you on as a copy boy."

Running copy on the *Journal*, personal copy jumper for Arthur Brisbane, head copy boy (and *only* copy boy) on the *New York Evening Graphic*, police reporter on the *Graphic*, the *Journal*, the *San Diego Sun*, journeyman reporter on dailies, weeklies, biweeklies throughout the country slowly structured a stockpile of characters, events and conflicting emotions without thought of making a film.

First brush with Hollywood was when MGM's offer of $5,000 (to fictionalize a solution to my bylined unsolved double-murder) was spurned because the City of New York offered $25,000 for a factual solution naming names. The murders are still unsolved. The corpses were wealthy, white-bearded, miserly octogenarian Edward Ridley and his male secretary. My lead was *Who Killed Santa Claus?* because Ridley loved foreclosing mortgages on Christmas. No regret turning down that $5,000. One day Who Killed Santa Claus will be my film contribution of a case of murder that defies solution yet maintains suspense to the empty end.

The question "Where do you get ideas for films?" isn't hard to answer.

Covering an execution . . . Told by a man who hacked his family to death with a meat cleaver on a Hudson River barge that he was sorry if he hurt them . . . Listening to a leaper's sex problem on a 30-foot ledge before he squashed a luckless passerby like a gnat . . . Extracting the identity of a blonde nude with paresis mounting a water hydrant singing the Star Spangled Banner because her name was Frances Key . . . Watching reporters refuse to help swing the tail of Lindy's plane at Teterboro Airfield in Jersey because they resented his reply to all their questions with "Is there anything else you want to ask?" . . . Breaking Jeanne Eagles' death by discovering her corpse in Campbell's Funeral Parlor . . . Posing for a Graphic composite of French flyers Nungesser and Coli in their wrecked plane in the ill-fated Atlantic hop only to baffle my mother who just couldn't understand that if the photographer was that close why the flyers weren't saved . . . Accompanying a rookie cop from the 24th Precinct on a routine complaint to stumble over a slain body in a subterranean office . . . Successfully interviewing J.P. Morgan only to watch my copy destroyed by the City Editor because he knew J.P. never granted interviews . . . Hired, fired, rehired by the great Gene Fowler in the span of five hours while assigned to an Admiral's speech that erupted miles away in a Bowery bum's brutal murder near Lum Fong's restaurant in Chinatown . . . Phoning blow-by- blow from a Harlem cigar store during a race riot . . . Using Sunday editions as bedsheets and blankets duding the rods with Depression displaced persons . . . Taking footbaths with hoboes in troughs of condemned milk . . . Drawing anti-chain market cartoons for a Rochester weekly while its Editor and Publisher ran for Governor of Minnesota to collect seven votes . . . Making caricatures of Texas cattle kings dropping manure from boots on the thick red rug in the Scarborough Hotel in Midland . . . Sketching whores in San Francisco while covering the General Strike as soldiers shot strikers in front of the Ferry Building . . . .

Every newspaperman has such a Hellbox to draw from.

Every newspaperman is a potential filmmaker.

All he has to do (or all she has to do) is to transfer real emotion to reel emotion and sprinkle with imagination.

This does not include critics. A newspaperman reports what happened, inwardly boiling with emotions that must remain personal. A critic outwardly reports what happened, writing what he liked or didn't like about the happening. Every story varies. A critic generally plays the same tune on his typewriter. A few have made it in films. Peter Bogdanovich stands out as one of that rare breed but he was more than a critic. He analyzed films the way a reporter analyzes emotions. He lifted himself out of the well of observer to creator.

My newspaper film Park Row was 1886 vintage because a passion for that street made the film a must. Drunk on stories of newspaper Goliaths before my time, hanging around Doc Perry's pharmacy in the *World* building where once Pulitzer picked up his medicine, working where once those Goliaths worked, walked, ate, drank, dreamed, fought, laughed and wept gave me selfish ejaculations when shooting the film on the stage replica of those paper-and-ink cobblestones.

Looking at the list of newspaper films to be screened, Five Star Final by Louis Weitzenkorn was based on Emile Gauvreau, Editor of the *Graphic*. Gauvreau gave Winchell his break. Also on that pink tabloid were Jerry Wald (radio editor), Norman Krasna (drama critic), Artie Auerbach (photographer) who became funny-man Mr. Kitzel on the Jack Benny Show, John Huston (reporter).

Weitzenkorn came from *The World* to replace Gauvreau who went to the *Mirror* to haunt Winchell, who loathed him. The changing of the Czars was macabre. Gauvreau's exit with a twisted foot, Weitzenkorn's entrance with a twisted arm. Abandoning Pulitzer to hit pornographic bottom on Bernard Macfadden's *Graphic*, Weitzenkorn struck playwright platinum: Gauvreau's exciting career.

Five Star Final's editor was factual. Gauvreau did updig an old murder, promised lurid revelations revealing the exonerated murderess's real name, terrified her. Result: the self-destruction of the woman and her husband. My role in that Bulldog bouillabaisse was to season it with facts on the son of the suicides. In the film it is the daughter. Gauvreau always washed his hands after a distasteful story. So does Edward G. Robinson in the film directed by Mervyn LeRoy.

Years later, when writing Gangs of New York, it was ironic to run into Weitzenkorn, who was writing a movie script called King of the Newsboys.

Seeing The Front Page play on opening night with Kermit Jaediker of the *New York Daily News* moved us because in Lee Tracy we saw what we were not but would like to be. It was thrilling. After the curtain came down it was back to the Press Room (a plumber's shop by day) across from the 47th Street Police Station and to the story of a grappling hook that finally brought up the body of a 5-year-old boy from the garbage in the Hudson. The beads of water on the eyelashes of the dead boy made me think of the beads of sweat on the brow of the unfortunate bastard that was hidden in the desk in The Front Page.

There is a tale that when Howard Hughes decided to film The Front Page he said "Get the man who's playing Hildy Johnson on the stage." Pat O'Brien was doing the role in Chicago. Hughes sent for him believing he was sending for Lee Tracy. True or not, it's a good story and Lewis Milestone who did a crackerjack job directing the film is the man who can confirm or deny the tale.

His Girl Friday was a superb sex-switch of The Front Page with breathtaking, machinegun tempo. After World War II the film became more personal to me because of Howard Hawks. My novel The Dark Page (purely a psychological study of an editor who commands a city-wide search for himself after murdering the wife he deserted 20 years ago) was written before World War II. The first draft was left with my mother who notified me in North Africa in the vicinity of Kasserine Pass that she spent the advance for the book she sold to publishers Duell, Sloan and Pearce. A hard cover of the book caught up with me in France near St. Lo, a Hollywood offer missed me in Mons, Belgium, and in Germany's Hurtgen Forest word was received that Howard Hawks bought the book for Bogart and Robinson for $15,000. He sold it to Columbia. It was filmed as Scandal Sheet with Broderick Crawford. That film is not my book.

Billy Wilder's The Big Carnival [Ace in the Hole] is the closest portrayal yet of a sonofabitch newspaperman. No punches pulled.

What takes place in a newspaper has yet to be filmed.

A newspaper – like a church, whore house, DAR meeting, political convention, KKK gathering, synagogue, American Legion Hall, public library – is a living character replated hourly with highly charged controversial nuances in every man and woman on the paper.

To make a real newspaper film is as difficult as to make a real war film. The censor is not the only barrier. People who buy tickets and walk into a peacock temple to crack pop corn in soft chairs have been doped over the years what war is like on the screen. They have been doped over the years what a newspaper is like on the screen.

Doped, duped, deluded – they know what to expect and will not accept a war film with indifference to atrocities, with combat verterans sacrificing wetnoses in a minefield, with the enjoyment of dehumanization, with the gall of brass referring to headless bodies as My Boys while in the sack with women in the rear, with distorted battle reports to grab votes, make loot, wave flags, sell arms, deal over burned and bloated corpses in the black market.

People will not accept a newspaper film with political atrocities and well-planned and paid-for character assassinations where names are accurate, they will not accept the cunning of the Desk blindfolding a reporter through a fog because he's on the verge of exposing a President, hurt an advertiser, jail a Federal Judge, disrobe a Vice Squad. They will not accept the FBI involved in blackmail because the FBI is the audience cracking pop corn. They will not accept publishers in theft with politicians, publishers whoring with bankers, profiting with big business, running meaningless Op-Ed letters against financial backers.

Past films have dealt with fictional exposés.

One day films will use *living names* in exposure.

100 years ago Washington politicians wouldn't give newspaper interviews unless they were paid. Today they pay ghosts to manufacture their autobiographies for a movie sale. Those auto-biographies never give damaging facts. Until the turn of the 18th century the Senate controlled newspaper exposés, thundering "Secrecy is the enemy of democracy!"

Today newspapers, *some* newspapers, publish Senatorial secrets that should be seen on the screen.

Trial by newspaper is still with us.

All the news that was unfit to print, all the scenes that were unfit to shoot, would make one hell of a newspaper film. It would have facts, legitimate characters, humor, shock, action. It would entertain and reveal. It would have the language of newspaper type spoken with flesh. It would show the passion of the printed word take on instant intimacy on film. It would go beyond the Bible, the newspaper, the stage. It would make words jump to life in shocking closeups. From Gutenberg to Griffith it would transfer from type to screen an accurate, shattering emotion of movement seen with eyes, heard with ears and never forgotten with the brain.

The true story of J. Edgar Hoover and the FBI would make a hell of a movie today. Not the year 1000. But today.

To make such a newspaper film I would give my right Linotype. Perhaps one day . . . soon . . . .At the moment am delerious with a new edition, the *first* edition in the family. My beautiful wife, actress Christa Lang, gave birth ot a beautiful girl named Samantha.

Right now Samantha is breast-fed.

Later she will be weaned on Mergenthaler and Films.

FROM THE FRONT PAGE TO THE FRONT PAGE

LOREN GHIGLIONE

In the opening act of Ben Hecht and Charles MacArthur's The Front Page, the Chicago police reporters needle Hildy Johnson, who has just quit reporting forever to marry and to enter advertising. Murphy of the *Journal* says: "I got a dumb brother went in for business. He's got seven kids and a mortgage, and belongs to a country club. He gets worse every year. Just a fathead."[1]

"Listen to who's talking," Johnson replies. "Journalists! Peeking through keyholes! Running after fire engines like a lot of coach dogs! Waking people up in the middle of the night to ask them what they think of Mussolini. Stealing pictures off old ladies of their daughters that get raped in Oak Park. A lot of lousy, daffy butinskis, swelling around with holes in their pants, borrowing nickels from office boys! And for what? So a milliion hired girls and motormen's wives'll know what's going on . . .. [Y]ou'll all end up on the copy desk – gray-headed, hump-backed slobs, dodging garnishees when you're ninety."[2]

Johnson's angry retort, however accurate, belies his love of reporting. By play's end, you know he'll be back in harness soon. Johnson's passion for reporting symbolizes the playwright's nostalgia for "the lusty, hoodlumesque half drunken caballero that was the newspaperman of our youth."[3] The Play's amusing portrait of the reporter – as wittily irreverent cynic and conniver determined to scoop the competition – has endured. The generation of real journalists dating from the 1960s may combine, as James Boylan writes, "the individualism and flair of The Front Page (that is, of yellow journalism) with the ideology and seriousness of 'professionalism.'"[4] But usually the professionalism gets left out of contemporary fiction, leaving The Front Page elements to define the journalist of today.

The continuing impact of The Front Page should not be a surprise. The 1928 play became a hit film in 1931. Other Hollywood versions followed: Rosalind Russell played a female Hildy Johnson in His Girl Friday (1940), Jack Lemmon acted the original part in a 1974 edition, and Kathleen Turner portrayed Hildy Johnson as a television reporter in Switching Channels (1988). A 1949-1950 television series – "The Front Page" set in a small town – cast CBS newsman John Daly as unscrupulous editor Walter Burns. Windy City, a musical version of the play, opened in 1982 with Dennis Waterman as Hildy Johnson.

New York revivals of The Front Page sell out every generation – 1946, 1968, and 1987 – and productions, amateur and professional, annually reintroduce the rascally reporters to new audiences across the country. The play's influence has extended to hundreds of newspaper movies and novels and plays in which reporters wear hats indoors, hide whiskey flasks in bottom desk drawers, wisecrack about cops, judges, and editors, especially editors, and display an all-consuming devotion to The Story.

Not that the reporter didn't exist in American fiction prior to 1928. The success of the nineteenth century penny press focused attention on the reporter who gathered the news. By 1871, a writer for *Lippincott's Magazine* could argue that "for the majority of readers it is the reporter, and not the editor, who is the ruling genius of the newspaper."[5]

The reporter piqued the public's interest. "There are few things concerning which the general public is more curious, and about which it knows less," Edwin Shuman wrote in his how-to guide, *Practical Journalism*, "than the inside of a metropolitan newspaper office."[6] Fiction romanticizing the work of the big-city reporter began to fill the void. The year 1890 saw the publication of the first novel devoted to reporting – Kirk Munroe's Under Orders: the Story of a Young Reporter – and a short story that was probably the most popular nineteenth-century fiction about the reporter.

Under Orders often reads like a simple blurb for journalism. "A first-class, well-trained reporter is one of the brightest, smartest, and best-informed men in the city," says Van Cleef, of the New York *Phonograph*. "He knows everybody worth knowing, and every thing that is happening or about to happen."[7] He also plays amateur detective. *Phonograph* reporter Myles Manning, the novel's hero, not only reports on an important railroad strike at Mountain Junction but discovers that villainous Ben Watkins plans to set fire to the railroad company office, making it appear strikers were to blame. Manning stops Watkins and achieves at novel's end a position as "foreign writer" for an influential illustrated magazine.

Richard Harding Davis's short story, Gallegher: a Newspaper Story (1890) sold more than fifty thousand copies when published in book form. It recorded the exploits of Gallegher, a Philadelphia *Press* office boy in whom "the detective element was abnormally developed."[8] Gallegher helps capture Hade, a notorious murderer. By lying to the police and stealing a horsedrawn carriage, Gallegher gets the story back to his paper before deadline . . . and before the competition. He proclaims, "I beat the town."[9]

Fiction from the early twentieth century painted a less upbeat picture of the reporter's life. Henry Beeker, the "reliable reporter"[10] in Ben Ames Williams's Splendor (1927), has no illusions: "I've been in the newspaper game long enough to know that most of the men who stick to it either die from overwork or go crazy or take to drinking or something."[11] Beeker's paper demotes him to the reference department.

Regret, in newspaper novels, often takes the form of a reporter's disappointment at not having tried to write the Great American Novel. In fact, Clyde Brion Davis, a newspaperman, wrote a novel entitled The Great American Novel – (1938). Despite his father's warning that newspapermen are "a drunken, shiftless lot of deadbeats,"[12] Homer Zigler becomes a reporter – and a drunken, shiftless deadbeat. His existence echoes a reporter's line in Thomas Wolfe's Gentlemen of the Press: "Christ! Maybe some day I'll write a book myself – about all the poor hams I've known in this game who were going to write a book – and never did. What a life!"[13]

But the public failed to be fascinated by the newspaperman trying to become a serious writer. "There are two kinds of newspaper-men," Ben Hecht explains in his novel Erik Dorn (1921), "those who try to write . . . and those who try to drink themselves to death. Fortunately for the world, only one of them succeeds."[14] The public responded, however, to the reporter who was a doer.

Isamu Noguchi's mammoth 1938 sculpture on the facade of the Associated Press building in New York captured the rushing movement – the energy and action – of the reporter. So did much fiction about the reporter as spy, adventurer, and, most important-ly, amateur detective.

The reporter and the detective both were considered hard-working and highly moral, even when breaking the law.[15] Both insisted on remaining loners and working by their own idiosyncratic rules.[16] And both mixed with high-hatters and the hoi polloi; they, like the heroes of Vern Partlow's song "Newspapermen" (1943), "wallo-w[ed] in corruption, crime, and gore."[17] To put the reporter and detective together in one person made for an ideal protagonist.

George Harmon Coxe, a former newspaperman, banged out mystery novels at the rate of three a year about newshounds, including photographers Kent Murdock and Jack "Flash" Casey, who worked as amateur detectives. Casey became the hero of a radio show, two motion pictures, and a television series with Darren McGavin. Heavy-drinking and handsome, "Flash" was given a personality that fitted many reporter-detectives. Coxe's description: "a quick impatience, especially with bores and phonies, a touch of irascibility too often quick to surface, a sharp and cutting tongue, frequently regretted, to express displeasure when some wrong, real or fancied, had been done, especially to those who lacked weapons to defend themselves."[18]

"Flash" Casey had plenty of company. Ronald Reagan starred as a boastful reporter-photographer in Nine Lives Are Not Enough (1941): "On the strength of my story and my story alone, he's behind bars."[19] Even Ernest Hemingway wrote a reporter-detective story (fortunately for Hemingway's literary reputation, the story remains unpublished).[20] The pulp magazines (including Front Page Stories and Newspaper Adventure Stories) featured Theodore Tinsley's Jerry Tracy, 'A Broadway wiseguy" gossip columnist,[21] Fred MacIssac's tramp reporter Addison Francis "Rambler" Murphy, and Richard Sale's breezy Joseph "Daffy" Dill. A typical Daffy Dill story opens: "When I came into the city room of the New York Chronicle I felt lower than a flounder's flatside, and I had a hangover that would have done credit to the old Romans of Bacchus' day."[22]

For children, board games – "Five Star Final" and "Scoop!" – and such stories as Mildred Benson's Dangerious Deadline (1957),[23] Norton Jonathan's Dan Hyland Police Reporter (1936),[24] and Walter R. Brooks's tales about Freddy the Pig[25] married reporting to sleuthing. Crime-solving comic-book superheroes – not only Superman (Clark Kent) – chose newspeople as their mortal identities. The roster of those superheroes reads like a guest list for a Halloween party: The Black Fury, The Ray, Bob Phantom, Captain Zero, The Crimson Avenger, The Destroyer, Elastic Lad, The Fox, Megaton Man, Miss America, Mr. A., Patriot, Son of Vulcan, Spider-Man, Spider-Ham, The Sword, and The Wasp.[26]

The Watergate reporting by the Washington Post's Robert Woodward and Carl Bernstein gave birth to All the President's Men (1975), a movie promoted as "The Most Devastating Detective Story of This Century." Novelists soon flooded bookstores with Washington investigative reporters, invariable winners of Pulitzer Prizes. Drew Pearson had previously provided Hap Hopper, a comic-strip crusader, but now Les Whitten, Jack Anderson's ferret, created Aubrey Warder of the Washington Eagle.[27] The Washington Post's Lawrence Meyer answered with reporter Paul Silver of the Washington Herald[28]. And Marc Olden created Harker, a Washington reporter for the New York World-Examiner, who had won two Pulitzers.[29] Perhaps the most blatant cloning of Woodstein occurred in Jeff Millar's Private Sector (1979). Millar's "perfect couple" – CBS-TV's John Harland and the New York Times's Molly Rice – saved the U.S. government from being taken over by two hundred mega-corporations.[30]

Molly Rice represented a growing interest in the woman gumshoe reporter stereotype. Minority reporters, however, rarely appeared in fiction.[31] African Americans were usually the victims of white reporters – as in Langston Hughes's "Name in Print"[32] – or journalistic Tontos to white Lone Ranger reporters and editors.

An exception – reporter Max Reddick in John A. Williams's The Man Who Cried I Am (1967) – works for a left-liberal New York newspaper and then a national newsmagazine where he is "a new Negro employee, a pioneer, a 'first Negro first.'"[33] Reddick began his career on the *Harlem Democrat*, interviewing Moses Lincoln Boatwright, a Harvard-educated African American who is finally executed for murdering and cannibalizing a white man. Boatwright had refused to tell white reporters the parts of the man he had eaten. Reddick receives a note from Boatwright written the afternoon before his execution: ". . . I took the heart and the genitals, for isn't that what life's all about, clawing the heart and balls out of the other guy?"[34]

In Arthur Hailey's Overload (1979) African American reporter Nancy Molineaux of the *California Examiner* stalks terrorists and Golden State Power and Light officials. She remains as independent and autonomous as any of her white male predecessors. "I know you prefer being a loner, and you've gotten away with it because you get results," growls Molineaux's city editor. "But you can push that game too far." Molineaux shrugs: "So fire me."[35]

While reporters have continued to be portrayed positively, cynicism toward all institutions – the press as well as Congress, religion, and business – has spawned fictional reporters who subvert the social order instead of defending it. Sometimes these anti-heroes or non-heroes lie to uncover the truth, but often they lie to lie. Sometimes they pursue the murderer, but occasionally they murder. In Jim Thompson's The Nothing Man (1954), Clinton "Brownie" Brown of the Pacific City *Courier* commits – or thinks he commits – the Sneering Slayer murders.[36] In the film Al Capone (1959), Keely, a sleazy reporter based on the Chicago *Tribune's* Jake Lingle, works for the Chicago mobster, double-crosses him, and winds up a corpse.[37]

Roger Simon's Wild Turkey (1974) presents a fictional version of *Rolling Stone* journalist Hunter S. Thompson. Gunther Thomas, "the renowned Ph.D. in guerilla journalism,"[38] smokes joints and lies thorough his bourbon breath. "I'll be back in twenty minutes . . . ." he says,[39] returning in thirteen months. Thompson wrote Fear and Loathing in Las Vegas (1971), which follows Raoul Duke on assignment with his three-hundred-pound Samoan Lawyer, Dr. Gonzo. Duke rents a red Chevrolet convertible, the Great Red Shark, and fills the trunk with acid, mescaline, cocaine, uppers, downers, and screamers. Duke plans to over a motorcycle and dune- buggy race as if it were the ultimate story, a Second Coming, "the American Dream"[40] – a search for "[f]ree lunch, final wisdom, total coverage."[41]

But Duke never actually reports anything, instead pumping himself full of drinks and drugs: "Why bother with newspapers . . .. Agnew was right. The press is a gang of cruel faggots. Journalism is not a profession or a trade. It is a cheap catch-all for fuckoffs and misfits – a false doorway to the backside of life, a filthy piss-ridden little hole nailed off by the building inspector, but just deep enough for a wino to curl up from the sidewalk and masturbate like a chimp in a zoo-cage."[42]

Gregory Mcdonald's Irwin Maurice Fletcher, the investigative reporter who stars in nine best-selling whodunits and two movies, represents the contemporary reporter. In Fletch (1974), the first novel in the series, Mcdonald's reporter works undercover as a beach bum on a drugs-amid-the-dunes investigation. He also tries to fathom millionaire Alan Stanwyk who, for fifty thousand dollars and a plane ticket to South America, wants Fletch to murder him.

To solve the two mysteries, Fletch, who describes himself as a liar with a magnificent memory, breaks all of journalism's rules. He pads his expense account with penicillin treatments for sex with strung-out druggies. He masquerades as a doctor, an insurance investigator, and reporter Bob Holson from the competing *Chronicle-Gazette*. In the end, Fletch cracks the drug ring, discovers Stanwyk is a murderer, and leaves the country with two attaché cases filled with three million dollars in tens and twenties.

Despite the drugs and other reminders of contemporary America, Mcdonald laces the Fletch mysteries with Front Page fun. Fletch skewers Clara, his news editor, with acerbic one-liners reminiscent of Hildy Johnson's assaults on Walter Burns. A police chief's routine questions also prompt wisecracks from Fletch. Police chief: "Do you live alone?" "Except for a pet roach." "And what do you do for a living . . .?" "I'm a shoeshine boy."[43] The portrayal of Fletch, like that of many fictional newshounds, owes less to real reporters than to the newsroom reprobates of The Front Page.

1. Ben Hecht and Charles MacArthur, The Front Page, (New York: Covici-Friede publishers, 1928), P.40.

2. Ibid., pp. 40-41.

3. Ibid., p. 31.

4. James Boylan, "Newspeople", in Philip S. Cook, Douglas Gomery, and Lawrence W. Lichty, eds., American Media: The Wilson Quarterly Reader (Washington: The Wilson Center Press, 1989), p. 62.

5. John Lesperance in Lippincott's Magazine, August 1871, Vol. VIII, p. 180.

6. Edwin L. Shuman, Practical Journalism: A Complete Manual of the Best Newspaper Methods (New York: D. Appleton and Co., 1903), p. vii.

7. Kirk Munroe, Under Orders: The Story of a Young Reporter (New York: G.P. Putnam's Sons, 1980), p.18.

8. Richard Harding Davis, Gallegher and Other Stories (New York: Charles Scribners's Sons, 1891), p.4.

9. Ibid., p. 57.

10. Ben Ames Williams, Splendor (New York: E. P. Dutton & Company, 1927), p. 120.

11. Ibid., p. 469.

12. Clyde Brion Davis, "The Great American Novel – –" (New York: Farrar Rinehart, 1938), p. 11.

13. Thomas Wolfe, "Gentlemen of the Press", in The Hills Beyond (New York: Harper & Row, Publishers, Inc., 1941; reprint, New York: New American Library, 1968), p. 52.

14. Ben Hecht, Erik Dorn (New York: The Modern Library, 1921), p. 20.

15. See Lee Wilkins, "Film as an Ethics", Journal of Mass Media Ethics, Vol. 2, No. 2 (Spring/Summer 1987), pp. 109-113; Steve Weinberg, "The Journalist in Novels", Journal of Mass Media Ethics, Vol. 2, No. 1 (Fall/Winter 1986-87), pp. 89-92; Deac Rossell, 'Hollywood and the Newsroom", American Film, October 1975, pp. 14-18.

16. Robin S. Winks talks about detectives working "sometimes against the grain of society". See Winks, Modus Operandi (Boston: David R. Godine, Publisher, 1982), p. 40.

17. See Vern Partlow, "Newspapermen", in Pete Seeger and Bob Reiser, Carry It On! A History in Song and Picture of the Working Men and Women of America (New York: Simon and Schuster, 1985), pp. 174-177.

18. Otto Penzler, ed., The Great Detectives (Boston: Little, Brown and Company, 1978), p. 43.

19. Alex Barris, Stop the Presses! The Newspaperman in American Films (South Brunswick, N. J.: A. S. Barnes and Company, Inc., 1976) p. 41.

20. Item 581, Hemingway Collection, John F. Kennedy Library. See also, Ronald Weber, "Journalism, Writing, and American Literature," Occasional Paper No. 5, April 1987, Gannett Center for Media Studies.

21. Theodore Tinsley as quoted in Ron Goulart, The Dime Detectives (New York: The Mysterious Press, 1988), p. 153.

22. Richard Sale, as quoted in ibid., p. 160,

23. Mildred Benson, Dangerous Deadline (New York: Dodd, Mead & Company, 1957).

24. Norton Jonathan, Dan Hyland, Police Reporter (Chicago: the Goldsmith Publishing Company, 1936).

25. See Walter R. Brooks, Freddy the Detective (New York: Alfred A. Knopf, 1932) and Freddy and the Bean Home News (New York: Alfred A. Knopf, 1943).

26. See Jeff Rovin, The Encyclopedia of Superheroes (New York: Facts on File Publications, 1985).

27. See Les Whitten, Conflict of Interest (New York: Doubleday & Co., 1976).

28. See Lawrence Meyer, A Capitol Crime (New York: The Viking Press, 1977) and False Front (New York, The Viking Press, 1979).

29. See Marc Olden The Harker File: Kill the Reporter (New York: Signet Books, New American Library, 1978).

30. See Jeff Millar, Private Sector (New York: The Dial Press, 1979).

31. See "Murder Between the Pages", in Victoria Nichols and Susan Thompson, Silk Stalkings: When Women Write of Murder (Berkeley: Black Lizard Books, 1988), pp. 161-179. For African American reporters in Film, see "Mystery in Swing" (1940), "The Red Menace" (1949), and "The Bedford Incident" (1965). Maxwell Taylor Courson, "The Newspaper Movies: An Analysis of the Rise and Decline of the News Gatherer as a Hero in American Motion Pictures, 1900-1974," (Ph.D. Dissertation, Cinema, University of Hawaii, 1976), says (p. 278): "[J]ournalism has enjoyed a whites-only image in Hollywood".

32. See Langston Hughes, "Name in Print", in John A. Williams, ed., The Angry Black (New York: Lancer Books, 1962). See also William Branch "A Medal for Willie", in Woodie King and Ron Miller, eds., Black Drama Anthology (New York: Signet/New American Library, Inc., 1972).

33. John A Williams, The Man Who Cried I Am (Boston: Little, Brown and Company, 1967), p. 240.

34. Ibid. p. 65.

35. Arthur Hailey, Overload (New York: Doubleday & Company, Inc., 1979), p. 270.

36. Jim Thompson, The Nothing Man, in Hard Core: 3 Novels (New York: Donald I. Fine, Inc., 1986).

37. Courson, op.cit., pp. 230-232.

38. Roger L. Simon, Wild Turkey (San Francisco: Straight Arrow Books, 1974), p. 1

39. Ibid., p. 2.

40. Hunter S. Thompson, Fear and Loathing in Las Vegas (New York: Popular Library, 1971), p. 6.

41. Ibid., P. 23. Elsewhere, Thompson refers to Fear & Loathing in Las Vegas as "a victim of its own conceptual schizophrenia, caught & finally crippled in that vain, academic limbo between 'journalism' and 'fiction' . . . a vile epitaph for the Drug Culture of the Sixties . . ." See Hunter S. Thompson, The Great Shark Hunt: Strange Tales from a Strange Time (New York: Summit Books, 1979), p.109.

42. Thompson, Fear and Loathing in Las Vegas, p. 200.

43. Gregory Mcdonald, "Fletch" in Fletch Forever (Garden City, N.Y.: Nelson Doubleday, Inc., 1978), p. 117.

FROM GOUDY TO GRIFFITH

The Fourth Estate and the Seventh Art in America

DEAC ROSSELL

"I am a mirror reflecting the spirit of the times," scandal-mongering columnist Ricardo Cortez declares in Is My Face Red? (William Seiler, 1932) the adaptation of newsmen Allen Rivken's and Ben Markson's play about an unscrupulous journalist unfetter-ed by considerations of propriety or good taste who breaks a murder story and finds himself embroiled with both the crooks and the police. In the first half of the century, movies and newspapers were the two great mass media, providing the American public with its daily and weekly diet of facts and fictions; in the second half they shared center stage with television, for which a good argument could be made that that electronic pipeline is in large part an amalgam of the two earlier media, with its reliance on news and information programming plus narrative genre entertainment.

Both newspapers and motion pictures served a largely urban public, one formed through immigration and internal migration at the turn of the century, and their mutual jealousies and passions led to a symbiotic relationship between the two media. The popular conception of the movies was transmitted to the public through endless stories, features, and stunts printed in the daily press, just as most Americans learned about the working life and journalistic issues of reporters through their representation on the silver screen. As the historian of early cinema Charles Musser observes, "The newspaper in turn-of-the-century America, then one of the few forms of mass communication, had a profound influence on other cultural practices, not least of which was the cinema."[1]

The earliest reporting on the new invention of motion pictures siezed on the invention's novelty and endorsed the medium as one showing great promise of educational utility. The Canastota *Bee* in small-town upstate New York, for example, wrote enthusiastically of the Biograph Company's new Mutoscope that "It will be of incalculable value to agents who wish to show customers the actual workings of intricate machinery and will amplify the scope of instruction in technical schools."[2] Enthusiasm for the new invention ran equally high in New York City, where the debut of Thomas Alva Edison's projecting Kinetoscope at Koster & Bial's Music Hall in Herald Square was called "intensely interesting and pleasing" by the New York *Herald* and "a decided hit" by the New York *Tribune*.[3]

After an initial flurry of reports on the new marvel, the novelty quickly wore off, and for the next five years there are few mentions of motion pictures in the press, as the early and ever-more imaginative claims of inventors for talking pictures, color pictures, and a television-like home dissemination of movies failed to materialize. Without much public notice in the daily press, and certainly without any regular coverage, the infant medium developed on its own as a storytelling entertainment.[4] Through the early 1900s movies developed rapidly in technique and in popularity, but their growth was mainly confined to working-class neighborhoods and immigrant audiences, well off the beat of middle-class newspapers. At this time, English literacy was the great watershed dividing these two powerful communicators. It is toward the end of the decade that the middle classes discover the existence of the movies, by then actively established as a burgeoning business and entertainment. It was then that the movies first felt the power of a reform-minded press, although a press often newly interested in building circulation in the growing urban neighborhoods. There the real story of the press and the pictures begins.

In March 1907, less than two years after the emergence of the nickeodeon, the five-cent theatre that was to provide entertainment for millions of working-class families, the Chicago *Tribune* suddenly editorialized against the popular new theatres in the strongest terms. The movies were considered to be "without a redeeming feature to warrant their existence," to be "ministering to the lowest passions of childhood." It was, said the *Tribune*, "proper to suppress them at once," and there "should be a law absolutely forbidding the entrance of a boy or girl under eighteen." In the final analysis the movies had no redeeming features: "[their] influence is wholly vicious . . . there is no voice raised to defend the majority of five cent theaters because they can not be defended. They are hopelessly bad."[5] At the time, Chicago had 116 nickelodeons, 18 ten-cent vaudeville houses and 19 penny arcades, all showing motion pictures.

The editorial caused a flurry of debate in Chicago throughout March, April and May of 1907, with reformer Jane Addams of Hull House presenting a resolution to the City Club on May 2, asking for regulation rather than suppression of movie theaters. Although it would take until November for Chicago's City Council to pass the nation's first censorship ordinance, the excitement of lambasting the new medium reached New York City on June 8, when Mayor George B. McClellan accepted a report from his police commissioner advocating the total suppression of all nickel theaters and arcades. All such licenses were abruptly revoked by the mayor after a crowded aldermanic meeting on December 24, 1907. This time news services carried the story of the shame of the motion picture across the country as if a new sport had been invented by some blustering Abner Doubleday.

This sequence of events in New York and Chicago was perhaps the first notice to the fledgling motion picture industry of the real power of the press. It was a far different arena – and with the closing of the nickelodeons in New York City, a far different effect – than the world of lawyers and law courts which had taken so much of moviemen's attention as they fought out the early patent wars and then defended their industry trust (the Motion Picture Patents Company) from the depradations of the independent picture makers. Moviemen suddenly had a real need to find some accommodation with this powerful voice in the community, one so evidently capable of influencing the shape and the very economic life of their newly-founded industry.

The accommodation with the press was not long in coming, and by ironic chance also came through initiatives of the Chicago *Tribune*. Circulation rivalries between the seven energetic Chicago newspapers had led, as one commentator delicately put it, "to the organization of armed camps. A complex conflict raged. The wagon bosses who delivered papers to the stands and the newsboys became remarkably persuasive." Until 1912, the *Tribune* had been an orthodox newspaper appealing to the upper classes and to literate readers under the capable leadership of the respected James Keeley. But Keely's star declined under two flamboyant young men who inherited the family fortunes controlling the *Tribune*, James Medill Patterson and Robert R. McCormick. At great expense, two staffers of the less prestigious *Evening American* came to the *Tribune:* Max Annenberg as circulation manager and the soon-to-be legendary Walter Howie as city editor.

Howie was the model Ben Hecht and Charles MacArthur used for the character of Walter Burns in their play The Front Page.[7] He and Annenberg believed that Chicago's newspaper-reading public demanded the most sensational and lurid treatment of the news. For their reporters, no tragedy was too private, no police-sealed room too secure, no testimony too secret to forestall a page one splash. Along with a Chicago movie producer, the Selig Polyscope Company, these two astute charlatans cooked up a scheme where the newspaper would run a serial story that would be seen simultaneously in movie theaters.

Loosely derived from the recent success of an Edison Company serial story called What Happened to Mary?, which had been used to promote circulation of the *Ladies World* magazine in early 1912, the result of the collaboration between Selig and the *Tribune* was the first genuine movie serial, The Adventures of Kathlyn, starring Kathlyn Williams and written for the newspaper by Harold MacGrath, an author of popular romantic fiction.

The *Tribune* now sought an audience amongst the patrons of the lowly nickelodeons, and they got one. The *Tribune* syndicated the story, the film was a popular success, and the paper's circulation rose by 50,000 readers, about 35,000 of whom became permanent readers. Annenberg and Howie's coup represented a boost of more than ten per cent in the newspaper's readership. Quickly, the idea was taken up as a basic element of the Chicago circulation wars, as well as elsewhere: on January 31, 1914 Edison released the first chapter of Dolly of the Dailies, syndicated in many newspapers; on April 4, the Universal Film Manufacturing Company released the first installment of Lucile Love, syndicated in the competing Chicago *Herald*; on April 11 the Eclectic Film company announced the release of The Perils of Pauline, syndicated through the Hearst newspapers, including the Chicago *Examiner*, which was directly competitive with the *Tribune*.

This flurry of activity was perhaps the first notice to the newspaper industry of the real popularity of motion pictures, and of the measurable gains accruing to those papers who found a viable relationship with this powerful new medium of entertainment. Newspapers could mobilize the populace. Movies could garner readership. Each had a product that was standardized yet ever-changing. Each had the habitual attention of millions of Americans. Each was in the process of extending the distribution of their product (stories/movies) to every city and town on a nationwide basis.

Although poet Vachel Lindsay published The Art of the Moving Picture in 1915, and Harvard's distinguished chairman of the Philosophical Department, Professor Hugo Munsterberg, issued The Photoplay: A Psychological Study in 1916, motion pictures and the bustling new urban newspapers both appealed to an unintellectual mass population. The motto of Patterson's New York *Daily News* (founded 1919) could serve as the slogan for attitudes of both the press and the pictures: "Tell it to Sweeney – The Stuyvesants will take care of themselves."

By the 1920s, when the movie moguls had organized the new

industry into the vertical monopoly of production, distribution and exhibition that produced the great Hollywood studios, a steady, dependable flow of films reached every city and town in America. And in parallel with this firmly established studio system the American newspaper developed a new and expanded film section. It contained news of the stars, news of forthcoming productions, 'reviews' of pictures playing in local theaters, feature stories, picture stories, interviews, fillers, announcements, contests, stunts, celebrity recipes, advice on grooming, and movie star gossip.

"It is under the heading of 'publicity' that the motion picture has probably reached its most individual development," said Robert H. Cochrane, Vice-President of Universal Pictures, to an audience at the Harvard Business School in 1927. "While publicity work can be defined as 'the dissemination of news' and the greater part of motion picture publicity is that and nothing more, it is nearer to the truth to define publicity work as the dissemination of *interesting reading matter*."[8] This daily repetition of "interesting reading matter" institutionalized the star system and laid the foundation for America's moviegoing habit, which reached 65 million weekly attendances in 1928, and 90 million in 1930 and again in 1946-48.

A relationship built on mutual need and mutual trust had begun and would remain unchanged for almost forty years. During the next decades many things would change in the movies themselves as stars rose and faded, genres gained and lost popularity, and new up-to-the minute themes replaced tired formulae, but the business and the information/publicity practice of the industry fundamentally stayed the same. The press agent who came to a newspaper in 1967 in a black suit, white shirt, necktie and neatly-trimmed head was the same man who arrived in 1971 with black jeans, open-necked black shirt, shoulder-length hair and moustache. Only the packaging had changed: the press and the pictures remained immutably tied together like the parallel iron rails of a roadbed extending into the distance.

Yet underneath the smoothly oiled machinery that each day filled the entertainment pages of the newspapers and the plush seats of the movie palaces, there remained a fundamental difference in the place of each industry in American culture. The United States Supreme Court, in its first encounter with motion pictures and freedom of speech, declared in the 1915 case Mutual Film Corporation v. Industrial Commission of Ohio that "It cannot be put out of view that the exhibition of moving pictures is a business pure and simple, originated and conducted for profit like other spectacles, not to be regarded, not intended to be regarded by the Ohio Constitution, we think, as part of the press of the country or as organs of public opinion. They are mere representations of events . . .."[9]

This decision, on a case involving prior-restraint mechanisms in one of the first state film censorship statutes, effectively separated films from such other 'businesses pure and simple' as book publishing and newspaper publishing. Both also conducted a business for profit, and the former, whether issuing works of greater or lesser merit, certainly engaged in the production of entertainment. By the 1950's, few decisions of the Supreme Court in the area of civil liberties had been more adversely criticized.[10] The traditional judicial suspicion of the arts in general is revealed in Mr. Justice McKenna's decision, with movies in particular called "more insidious in corruption" since they were ordinarily shown to mixed audiences of adults and to children of both sexes.[11]

The damage was done. The wording and weight of the decision had a profound effect on the film industry, as many courts interpreted the will of the Supreme Court to be that motion pictures were excluded from any protections of state or Federal guarantees of free speech.[12] From 1915 the movies had no recourse in the courts and no respectability. Ever after, the moguls of the studios and their colleagues right down to the local theatre managers lusted after respectability as intensely as they did after the mountains of cash piling up in their box offices. In their partnership with the press, the moviemen remained abidingly jealous of the freedom of expression and legal protections given to newspaper reporters.

Although it is clear that motion pictures are often a powerful tool for the dissemination of ideas and the persuasion of the public, this early decision relegated them to the weakest of legal and cultural positions in any potential defense of their content or of their conduct in advocating ideas. The movies had no recourse in the courts, as did newspapers with their constitutional protections, and no respectability. When Will Hays was brought into the film industry to establish the self-regulating Motion Picture Code, thereby heading off a movement towards a national censorship office, the prelude to the Code read like a defensive replay of the Mutual case: "Motion picture producers . . . though regarding motion pictures primarily as an entertainment without any explicit purpose of teaching or propaganda, know that the motion picture within its own field of entertainment may be directly responsible for spiritual or moral progress, for higher types of social life, and for much correct thinking."[13]

If movie producers remained covetous of the freedoms of their colleague newspaper publishers, they had in excess something that newspaper reporters saw infrequently, if at all: very large sums of money. Herman J. Mankiewicz's famous 1925 telegram to the broke and congenial former Chicago newspaper colleague Ben Hecht tells the whole story: "Will you accept three hundred per week to work for Paramount Pictures? All expenses paid. The three hundred is peanuts. Millions are to be grabbed out here and your only competition is idiots. Don't let this get around." A newspaper photograph shows Mankiewicz greeting the "noted author, dramatist, and former newspaperman" Hecht on his quickly-arranged arrival in Hollywood. As if it were not enough to have a job at a pay scale far above the journalistic salaries of the day, Hecht records that it took him a whole week to produce the screenplay for Josef von Sternberg's Underworld, the director's first hit and Hecht's first Oscar-winning film. "I was given a ten-thousand dollar check as a bonus for the week's work," Hecht recalled in his autobiography.[14]

No single profession provided a larger or steadier stream of workers for the film community than the profession of newspapering.

Hundreds of jouralists wrote, directed, or produced thousands of films. In the pioneering days of the movies, Bannister Merwin and Charles Henri France at Edison's studio had newspaper experience, as did J. Stuart Blackton and George D. Baker at Vitagraph, directors Arthur Hotaling and George Terwilliger at Lubin, Travers Vale at Biograph and later World, Lois Weber at Universal, George Brackett Seitz at Pathé, Henry McRae at Essanay, and Richard F. Jones at Keystone. They were only the advance guard of a constantly changing cast of reporters and editors who tried their hand at movie life, drawn by the glamor, money, fame, or the plain certainty that the skills that produced page one were fully compatible with the rewards of producing reel one.

And the newsmen and women who stayed at home were equally under the thrall of the new movie medium and the thrall that it held over the public's imagination throughout the 1920s and 1930s. Journalists on the motion picture and entertainment beats took a cue from the Hollywood stars and adapted their own mellifluous pseudonyms for their columns: just as Lucille Vasconellos Langhanke became Mary Astor, Mrs. G. A. Flaskick of *The Enterprise* in Beaumont, Texas, became Betty Browne; as Samuel Jones Grundy became Wallace Ford on the screen, Earl L. Borg of the *Desert News* in Salt Lake City became Scott Boutywell.

In order to help newspapers "learn" about the movies, distributors and producers created an elaborate system for hand feeding information to the press. Helped by the fact that most of the movie company staffers doing the feeding had come from behind the same desks, telephones, and typewriters that they were now trying to shill, albeit at significantly higher salaries, the movies developed the art of publicity into a fine art. "In fact," noted Robert Cochrane, "the motion picture publicity man is a reporter working for the newspapers and magazines of the country. In operation, the publicity chief of a large company is a managing editor, with a staff of news gatherers, special writers, and photographers sufficiently large to get out a good-sized paper."[15]

In the recollection of veteran film publicist Arthur Mayer,

Cochrane's analogy between publicity men and reporters was almost too true for some New York critics in the 1920s. The press agent for the Rialto Theatre when it was operated by the preeminent showman Samuel Lionel Rothafel, known as Roxy, was none other than Terry Ramsaye, the pioneer film historian and trade publisher. Ramsaye found a new way to use the leverage of the press in the never-ending battle between exhibitors who wanted low rental rates for films, and distributors who wanted to maximize their own profits with high rates. According to Mayer, Ramsaye "wrote reviews of forthcoming pictures and gave them to the newspapers, whose representatives in those days greatly appreciated having their work done for them. Most of Ramsaye's reviews were favorable, even on occasions when the pictures were only passable, but when the film rentals were still in dispute, he would pan them mercilessly. Several distributors were guided in this manner to see the light."[16]

Movie companies have always been the journalist's primary source of information about individual films, players, and changes in the business. Whether the press took reviews complete, or rewrote publicity material as if it had come from a wire service, until the late 1960s there was rarely the will or the opportunity to check facts independently and to verify industry accounts of the happenings inside Hollywood. Extremely rare is the newspaper office that keeps an independent library of film references beyond their own clippings; in most cases there are no independently produced reference materials about current films coming into release. Comfortably wrapped in a seeming intimacy with the stars, supplied with voluminous "interesting reading matter," and periodically flown from city to city for staged publicity events, screenings, and round-robin interviews, the press never achieved, and never really sought independence from their symbiotic colleagues in the movies.

Given the highly controlled access to information and personalities within the movie business, steps toward independence by a journalist could be costly, and the pressures on the reporter were both internal and external. When this writer printed a 'wrong' picture of Charlton Heston after an interview in 1969, United Artists Pictures Corp. denied the paper access to screenings and materials for three months, while supplying four competing journals. On the other hand, one major critic at a declining Boston daily, whose publisher was frantically seeing younger readers in that university-dominated community found herself regularly conflict with the paper's advertising manager as she wrote about a new foreign film opening for the college trade in Cambridge. Raging that the theatre "did not advertise" he would storm into her office and extract a promise, always broken in another few months, that the critic would never again "publicize" a theatre which did not have a steady advertising account. That paper is now dead.[17]

As much as the film industry can try to control access to information and personalities, to put the appropriate "spin" on facts, and to purvey "interesting reading matter," Hollywood professionals know that they cannot continue to reach the public without a widespread and continual relationship to the news media. Like reportorial work on the city desk and elsewhere, then, each story becomes a protracted negotiation over access to individuals, content, timing, and placement, in the best possible light seen from two opposing viewpoints: the publicist who seeks uncritical, often flamboyant space giving notice to a picture, and the reporter seeking to inform the paper's readers. It is easy for principles on either side of the equation to slip, leaving movie personalities exceedingly vulnerable to the whims and journalistic standards of writers and editors.

When actress Karen Black (Day of the Locust, Family Plot) married writer Kit Carson, newspapers across the U.S. had just been reporting the quick marriage-and-separation of two other celebrities, Gregg Allman and Cher. Picking up on this national gossip, one newspaper ran "quotes" from both Black and Carson about their own quick separation on their wedding night, as Black purportedly flew to New York from Calfornia to close a movie deal. Her eagerness to go on with her career would separate the couple for several days, and the "quotes" recounted the difficulties of celebrity marriage. Patently untrue – the couple had dinner the night of their marriage with this writer and his wife in a small restaurant high in the hills over Hollywood – and with no separation at that time at all, Black and Carson had no defense to this invasion of privacy, no recourse to the public. The studios and the personalities who so ardenly seek and so need the printed media to continue their business and their careers are fully at the mercy of the press and of its standards of professionalism and conduct.

These examples suggest that a cynical pragmatism suffuses the operations of the American newspaper, a spirit caught frequently in the newspaper films of the 1930s. As Max Lerner noted, the American press is "not oriented toward inner life, but toward an outward one in which almost anything can happen to give a decisive turn to life."[18] The same emphasis on event without context, fact separated from philosophy, is central to the American film. With theatre programs changing weekly, American movies were geared to a production pace that made last month's film as passé as last week's newspaper. The star system, with its pressure for a leading player to portray repetitively a minimally differentiated character in a multitude of films is analogous to the journalistic habit of repetitively covering a limited number of beats within a well-defined range of subjects.

American films reflect a penchant of doing basic to American civilization: films are about active people, makers, movers, shakers, accomplishers. Ben Hur. Charles Foster Kane. Virgil Tibbs. Indiana Jones. The genres of accomplishment where the individual triumphs are the uniquely American genres: crime pictures, westerns, spy stories, newspaper films. And typically, that other uniquely American film genre, the musical film, also deals with accomplishment as a chorus girl becomes a star.

Motion pictures seized on newspapers as a primary conduit for expressing the values of accomplishment in American society from their earliest days. The tradition of the crusading newspaper, perhaps best exemplified by Joseph Pulitzer's St. Louis *Post-Dispatch*, became a natural expression of the pragmatism inherent in the American film. Before World War I, movie reporters were seen as they struggled for the scoop on a train wreck story (Tapped Wires, 1913), foiled graft in city street work (The Grafters, 1913), vindicated an innocent man by capturing a counterfeiter (The Power of the Press, 1914). In the same era female reporters exposed collusion between politicians and a big utility (The Reform Candidate, 1911) and exposed corruption in a city administration (Her Big Story, 1913).

The movies quickly found that any kind of story could be built around a reporter as the central character. While Pauline Kael has accurately pointed out that American films rarely show a character at work, the job of a newspaper reporter was so mobile and his working office so intriguing that the newspaper film genre is the one glaring exception to the rule. The reporter has mobility through society, has an activist motivation to solve problems and find out the truth, has friends of all social classes and in all places. The reporter is on the inside and knows what the public does not know about power structures and the private lives of public figures. The reporter has an excellent memory, and often uses his or her impeccable recall to further justice. And yet the reporter is human and can have the same loves, hates, prejudices, romances, ego, and desires as common folk. The reporter has free time and free access across town, and is rarely shown writing. According to legend, the reporter works twenty-four hours a day, finding information in unlikely places from unlikely people at unlikely times. The reporter is a center of power, backed by his publication – or if not, at least by constitutional ideals – and is sought out by persons of all types because the reporter can generate publicity or information or fix something up among his or her regular contacts at city hall and the station house.

Throughout the 1920s the movies treated the press with a combination of naïveté and enthusiasm. There are films about reporters catching crooks (Dangerous Traffic, 1926), reporters defeating political machines (What a Night, 1928), reporters volunteering to help the good works of a mission (The Day of Faith, 1923), reporters protecting a woman's reputation (Her Reputation, 1923), reporters exposing the decadence of high society

(Salome of the Tenements, 1925); the purifying vocation of journalism is so remarkable that there is even a film where a crook reforms by buying a newspaper and turning it against his former colleagues (The Man Under Cover, 1922). One reviewer wrote a not untypical comment on The Last Edition (1925) a film that used the interior of the San Francisco *Chronicle* plant for much of its background to the story of a composing room foreman who breaks a political scandal: "The picture gives an unusually clear idea of the thought and action involved in bringing out a newspaper. The work in different departments, such as the city room, the composing room, and the pressroom are exceptionally well filmed, and the scenes for 'making over' for an extra edition are decidedly impressive."[19]

Throughout the 1920s the reporter remained essentially a man or woman of action, a problem-solving figure working for the god of society as a whole. The moral virtue of the newsman remained largely unquestioned until the 1930s, when a remarkable series of films began to question the freedoms of the press and the responsibilities of the reporter. A new generation of reporters went to Hollywood to write dialogue fo the new talking pictures, and they often based their newspaper films on their own experiences or those of their colleagues. These experiences often had a more questionable moral tone, and an ideology of the press began to be represented in public for the first time on a broad populist scale. Against the background of the play and first film version of The Front Page, three 1932 films were only the beginnings of a cycle based loosely on the career of Walter Winchell (Okay, America; Is My Face Red?; and Love is a Racket). These films helped confirm the unredeemed cynicism, staccato dialogue, snap-brim hats worn indoors, and the quick wisecrack that became the essential elements of the reporters in the genre. This new cycle introduced "the types of reporters who sit on the edge of the publisher's desk" (Sued for Libel, 1940); editors who were "a cross between a Ferris Wheel and a werewolf" (Nothing Sacred, 1937); and reporters described by their editors as "cynical, crazy, drunken bum[s]" (Murder Man, 1935). One of Lee Tracy's many portrayals of the nervy, finger-popping reporter had him nicknamed "Ego", while Ricardo Cortez in is My Face Red? boasted "I'm the guy that made Broadway famous!" Mervyn LeRoy's bitter portrait of scandalmongering, Five Star Final (1931), pulled no punches in its attack on yellow journalism and the excesses of the press. And the public came to realize that the reporter was not a simple defender of the common man, but many would stop at nothing to get a story and build the circulation of their papers.

Back on the City Desk, the perpetual momentum of the Hollywood publicity machines grinding out "interesting reading matter" seems to have smothered any real outcry from the press at their portrayal in the movies. Critical comments frequently revealed a suppressed longing to joining their colleagues on the parade west to Los Angeles. "From a newspaperman's viewpoint," wrote John T. McManus of the New York Times in reviewing Missing Girls, "there is less to carp about in Roger Pryor's screen reporter characterization than there has been in similar representations by better known players. He doesn't, for example, dictate headlines over the telephone. We did hear him set a social engagement for 8 o'clock in the evening once, however, and that is something we've never been able to do."[20] The year before, André Sennwald wrote in the same paper: "It is one of this department's favorite themes that films which distort the newspaper profession in their efforts to convey the clamor of that fascinating craft are always written by former newspaper men. Somehow, when the boys clean out their desks and sell out to the Mecca of the Pacific, they quickly forget the realities of the city room and proceed to simonize their fiction with the dreams that never came true when they were taking orders from the city desk."[21]

Not all of the 1930s films were critical of the role of the press and the methods of reporters. The newspaper reporter on film remained in most cases a mobile hero ready for comedy, romance and action. From It Happened One Night (1934) to Front Page Woman (1935) and Wife Versus Secretary (1936), dozens of films used the public's familiar expectations of the glamorous reporter as the basis for a wide range of film productions. The most unusual aspect of these films was the opportunities they accorded to women.

Beginning in 1911 (The Reform Candidate), continuing throughout the 1920s (The Green Flame, 1920; The Whispered Name, 1924; A Woman Against the World, 1928) and coming to full flower in the 1930s (Sob Sister, 1931; Front Page Woman, 1935; Smart Blonde, 1937) the newspaper film genre was the only place where an actress could portray a role that stood on an equal footing with men. Reduced to a symbol of personal power in the gangster film, and to a symbol of civilization playing the schoolteachers and reformers in the western, in the newspaper films a woman could take the lead, be the active protagonist, catch the crooks, save the day, scheme for power, find success on her own terms and move independently through society. Joan Crawford saves her brother and earns the respect of her colleagues by catching gangsters in Dance, Fools, Dance (1931). Constance Bennett resolves a scandal in a prominent family in After Office Hours (1935). Joan Bennett as a manicurist-turned-reporter/editor cleans up a town in Big Brown Eyes (1936). Katharine Hepburn fights Victorian conventions and seeks independence in A Woman Rebels (1936). When Rosalind Russell burst into the office of her editor, Cary Grant, in Howard Hawks's His Girl Friday (1940), she was tangoing down a well-worn pathway. By 1940 women reporters were commonplace and approved in the eyes of both Hollywood and the public. Throughout the 1930s major actresses seeking roles with more independence, with a career background, and with more than romantic motivations suddenly became newspaperwomen: in addition to Russell, Hepburn and Davis, there was Joan Crawford (Dance, Fools, Dance, 1931); Loretta Young (Platinum Blonde, 1931); Virginia Bruce (Murder Man, 1935); and the female answer to Lee Tracy in the person of Glenda Farrell, who starred in all but one of the seven Torchy Blane pictures about an enterprising newspaperwoman.

After World War II, the galamour went out of newspaper films, and simultaneously the relationship between the press and the pictures began slowly to dissolve. Many of the best newspaper films had been created as fond reminiscences of lost youth by men and women graduated from the world of newswriting to screenwriting. As these talents began to move to the fringe of the film industry, itself challenged by television to make bigger and more costly widescreen films and to reduce the number of quick, cheap, spare B films in release, the newspaper film genre slowly began to dissipate.

A few remarkable productions continued to appear: Samuel Fuller's idealistic paen to free journalism, Park Row (1952), which he called "the story of my heart'; Billy Wilder's bitter indictment of inhuman reportorial excess, Ace in the Hole (1951), with its brilliant performance by Kirk Douglas; Jack Webb's intriguiging attempt to portray one day in the working life of a small town paper — —30— — (1959, also known as Deadline Midnight). Slowly, the reporter became a sidebar figure. Instead of the central, gangling, iridescent Lee Tracy, the elegant Adolphe Menjou, or the debonaire Cary Grant, the reporter was reduced to a confused David Janssen, a propped-up, weak, squeamish, cardboard figure of false liberalism who hung around the edges of a picture waiting to be told the real story by conservative, arch-right heroes like John Wayne in a series of films including Shoes of the Fisherman (1968), The Green Berets (1968), and Marooned (1969).

In 1972, hypnotic national attention (and debate) attended the ongoing revelations of Watergate shennannigins in the press, led by the work of two young reporters, Carl Bernstein and Robert Woodward of the Washington *Post*. This story, later memorialized in Alan J. Pakula's film All the President's Men (1975), re-glamourized the profession of reporting, and opened the door to the production of an occasional crusading newspaper film, including Under Fire (1983, on Central America), The Killing Fields (1984, on Cambodia), Salvador (1986, on El Salvador), and Cry Freedom (1986, on South Africa). But through the 1960s and 1970s, with fewer papers printing fewer editions in smaller sizes, and Hollywood making fewer movies on more daring themes for larger production budgets, the special relationship between the pictures and the press began to break up. The stunts and gossip and recipes; and casting announcments were crowded out of newspapers. With fewer pictures in release each year producers attached more and more importance to each review and each mention in print, and newspapers felt pressured. The movie companies were still paying top dollar for their advertising, and resented the shrinking copy space in papers for whom the huge growth of professional sports was now the main object of gaining and retaining mass circulation.

With both media under increasing pressure from a tightening economy, separate sets of difficult unions, and a public turning more frequently to television for its news and its entertainment, the party of the decades between the wars was over. For half a century through 1960, the press and the pictures were tied in a closely watched, mutually useful and uniquely powerful alliance which shaped American culture and American consciousness. If today this alliance is broken, mediated by television and home videotape retailling, it is still instructive to remember the words of the trade paper *Moving Picture World*, which editorialized at the beginning of the era in words that now seem prophetic. After delivering a sermonette on fair and impartial criticism, the editors wrote that this new form of entertainment was in a state where ". . . the possibilities of which are only just being revealed. For the moving picture will last just as long as the newspaper . . .."[22]

— — 30 — —

1. Musser, Charles: Before the Nickelodeon: Edwin S. Porter and the Edison Manufacturing Company (Berkeley, 1991: University of California Press), p. 10. Discussing early cinema practice as a form of visual newspaper, Musser continues: "Individual films had strong ties to different types of journalistic features: news stories, editorial cartoons, human interest columns, and the comic strip. Even fight films and travel scenes were not inconsistent with cinema as a visual newspaper, for the papers covered both sports and travel. As with the newspapers, the purpose of cinema at the turn of the century was to inform as much as to entertain."

2. The Canastota *Bee*, August 5, 1895, p. 1.

3. Both May 3, 1896. An earlier press report of Edison's work perhaps illustrates the first example of commercial influence over press reporting of the movies. On May 30, 1981, both newspapers in Orange, New Jersey, where Edison's laboratory was located, reported that the Wizard was at work on a device to reproduce motion photographically. The Orange *Chronicle*, which got Edison's printing business, gave the story half a column on page one, while the Orange *Journal*, which didn't get Edison business, buried the story on a back page.

4. See Charles Musser, Before the Nickelodeon: Edwin S. Porter and the Edison Manufacturing Company (Berkleley, 1991: University of California Press), p. 9-11. "By

1902-3, cinema was losing its efficacy as a visual newspaper and was reconceived primarily as a storytelling form." (p. 10)

5. Chicago *Tribune*, March 12, 1907, p. 8.

6. Terry Ramsaye, A Million and One Nights (New York: Simon and Schuster, 1926), p. 657.

7. Contradictory to many published reports, Ben Hecht never worked for Howie, "being incapable of such treachery as he proposed."

8. Robert H. Cochrane, "Motion Picture Publicity" in Joseph P. Kennedy, ed., The Story of the Films (Chicago: A. W. Shaw and Company, 1927), p. 238. Emphasis in original.

9. 236 U.S. 230 (1915), Mutual Film Corporation v. Industrial Commission of Ohio, p. 244.

10. See especially "Motion Pictures and the First Amendment," Yale Law Journal 60, (1951), p. 696-719.

11. 236 U.S. 230 (1915), above, p. 246.

12. The Mutual case was not overturned until 1952 in 343 U.S. 495, Burstyn v. Williams, fought over the Roberto Rossellini film The Miracle. Here the Court specifically rejected the 1915 judgement: "We no longer adhere to it." See especially C. Herman Pritchett, Civil Liberties and the Vinson Court, (Chicago: University of Chicago Press, 1954), pp. 412ff.

13. Raymond Moley, The Hays Office (Indianapolis:; 1945, The Bobbs-Merrill Company), p. 241.

14. Ben Hecht, A Child of the Century (New York, 1954: Simon and Schuster), p. 448.

15. Kennedy, op. cit., p. 240.

16. Arthur Mayer, Merely Colossal (New York, 1953: Simon and Schuster), p. 185.

17. Habitually in the U.S., entertainment advertising (theatre, movies, music, etc.) commands the highest per-line advertising cost in the paper, with general merchandise department stores having the lowest rates. This curious tradition may have developed out of the experiences of 19th century travelling theatre and vaudeville groups, notorious for skipping town without paying their bills (and often their players). Non-resident in the community, ads for such travelling shows were charged high rates which represented extra money to the local papers, always paid in cash with no credit extended. The tradition of a high rate continues to this day.

18. Max Lerner, America as a Civilization (New York, 1957: Simon and Schuster), vol. 2, p. 749.

19. (unsigned) The New York *Times*, November 11, 1925, p. 22.

20. John T. McManus, review of "Missing Girls", The New York *Times*, October 5, 1936, p. 33.

21. André Sennwald, review of "The Pay-Off", the New York *Times*, November 13, 1935, p. 23.

22. Moving Picture World, March 20, 1909, p. 3.

THE NEWSHAWKS

Peter Roffman and Jim Purdy

The two major journalistic trends of the early thirties were a proliferation of serious political commentary and a greater predilection for sensationalist copy. The syndicated columns of Walter Lipmann, Heywood Broun, Mark Sullivan, and Arthur Brisbane satisfied a new social awareness on the part of newspaper readers, a desire to make sense of the confusing events of the day. Heightened preoccupation with lurid crime and scandal (the Lindbergh kidnapping, numerous gangland murders, etc.) gave rise to another, less wholesome, tendency: a voracious appetite for stories about corruption and murder. The writers of such stories, the muckrakers and the gossip columnists, became popular in their own right. Personalities such as Drew Pearson and Walter Winchell seemed to have a ringside seat on the events of the day and be part of the sin they reported.

Hollywood was of course far more interested in the sensationalist trend than in serious political commentary. In raiding the headlines for story material and importing many journalists as screenwriters, it was inevitable that the movies discovered the affinities between the columnists' public image and that of the shyster. Soon the reporter was incorporated into the shyster's crooked city world. Like the lawyers and politicos, he at first appeared only as a minor figure on the fringe of the underworld, as one of the hangers-on who follow the gangster and report his antics to an eager public. Before long he emerged as the hero of his own popular series (at least ten films between 1931 and 1933).

The reporter perfectly embodies the shyster qualities. A tough, fast-talking cynic who prowls about unchecked in a corrupt world, continually on the lookout for trouble and a good story, he moves with speed and assurance – immediately on the scene of a news event to scoop the other papers, furiously typing out his story amidst the hustle and bustle of the newsroom. The urgency and dynamism of the world is best illustrated by the movies' dialogue (often written by ex-journalists like Hecht and MacArthur). No one talks faster than the reporters[1] and the rapid-fire wisecracks and overlapping cut-ups create a hyped-up comic velocity, a kind of verbal slapstick. The reporters are lovable roustabouts, as smooth and charming as the lawyers while at the same time somewhat rowdy and vulgar. As Hecht and MacArthur describe him, the reporter of these films is "the lusty, hoodlumesque half-drunken caballero who was the newspaperman of our youth."[2]

As usual, the shyster figure's main attraction is his cynicism. The newsman's assumptions are based on shyster society: he just takes for granted that there is corruption, that someone is on the take, and of course, he's always proven correct. The basis of his appeal is that he judges society accurately and acts accordingly. His inside knowledge of its dirty workings makes the reporter a master of the corrupt city world, but also makes him a part of it, for amorality is a necessary requisite for survival. Hecht and MacArthur comment on Walter Burns: "Mr. Burns is that product of thoughtless, pointless, nerve-drumming immorality that is the Boss Journalist – the licensed eavesdropper, trouble maker, bombinator and Town Snitch, misnamed The Press."[3] Being a part of the evil and at the same time above it, the reporter, like all shysters, combines the illicit appeal of sin with the moral righteousness of superiority.

Amorality is both an alluring and an effective modus operandi. Lacking any scruples or sentiment, the reporter is able to manipulate all situations and feel at home everywhere. He simultaneously outwits gangsters, evades police, and competes against rival papers trying to butt in on his scoop. No matter whom he confronts or what the circumstances, the journalist never fails to have a glib comeback and another devious trick up his sleeve. The Front Page (1931) provides the classic example of the reporter matching wits on all sides. Editor Walter Burns (Adolphe Menjou) and star newshawk Hildy Johnston (Pat O'Brien) conceal an escaped criminal from everyone – rival journalists, the police and the mayor, even Hildy's future mother-in-law – all while they try to get a story ready for the press and Hildy tries to patch up his disintegrating wedding plans. Blessed Event (1932) sees its columnist hero Alvin Roberts (Lee Tracy, who most frequently appeared in this cycle, having first gained attention in the stage version of The Front Page) continue to print scandalous stories despite various attempts on his life. When a fearsome gangster confronts him over remarks in his column, it is the nervy reporter who ends up intimidating the armed thug. In Is My Face Red? (1932) William Poster (Ricardo Cortez) is so much in the know that he can announce a murder in his column before the police have even discovered the body. The audience could easily identify with a hero whose success depended on his being tougher and less scrupulous than anyone else.

The reporter is willing to go to any lengths to get a story and boost his paper. Randall (Edward G. Robinson), the editor in Five Star Final (1931), has his staff use whatever deceit and subterfuge are necessary to dig up the facts of a long-forgotten sex murder. The paper's ace sleuth, Isabod (Boris Karloff), obtains an intertview with the now repentant murderess and her husband by posing as the minister who is to officiate at their daughter's wedding. In The Front Page, Burns does everything to spoil Hildy's wedding because he doesn't want to lose his star reporter. In the famous ending, after he finally gives Hildy his blessings and his own watch as a wedding gift, Walter phones the police to have him arrested: "The son of a (blurred) stole my watch!"

The truth too is malleable. If it means more dramatic headlines, the journalist will not hesitate to twist the facts. In The Front Page, the press distort the case of Earl Williams (George E. Stone), portraying the timid and gentle man as a vicious killer because it sells better. Having just witnessed Williams meekly surrender to the police, the newsmen hastily rush to phone in stories to their papers. On seven phones there are seven different versions of the same event: "Williams put up a desperate struggle but the police overpowered him," "Williams was unconscious . . .," "A well-dressed society woman tipped off the cops," "An old sweetheart of Williams double-crossed him."

Quite often the reporter is closely tied to the gangster. He either uses him when violence proves necessary (Walter has "Louie" kidnap Hildy's mother-in-law) or feeds off his lawlessness, exploiting the popularity of the gangster's adventures. In effect, the reporter is doing what Hollywood movies do, glorifying crime and sensationalizing violence for an eager audience. In The Secret Six glib newspaperman Carl (Clark Gable) is complicit in Scorpio's rise to power. Accepting gifts from the gangster, he lionizes him in the press and thereby helps his stooge win the mayoralty race. The police chief denounces him for the same reason many Hollywood movies were attacked: "And you newspaper guys. Making heroes out of these bums."

As the conventions dictate, the reporter reforms and always ends up on the side of the law. But the reporter's reformation is seldom as self-righteous as that of the lawyers and Doc Varney; indeed, it hardly diminishes his cynicism or illicit appeal. He never really undergoes a change of heart and even when he wants to quit, he finds it impossible to leave his work. Despite Hildy's denunciation of the journalistic profession and his avowed intention to get married and go into another business, he drops everything, including his girl, at the first scent of a story. Journalism is in the reporter's blood and no moral reformation can either quench his thirst for amorality or (with some exceptions) impel him to leave the sin behind. Instead he continues to satisfy his own personal needs and by the dramatic climax those needs inevitably coincide with those of the law. Carl helps bring Scorpio down and goes on to lead a campaign to "clean up" the country. Yet throughout it all he retains his cool independence and fast-talking rascality. There is little hint of social idealism behind Walter and Hildy's exposé of the city's corrupt mayor and police chief. Their real concern is in getting the story exclusively, to say nothing of beating the rap for harboring a criminal. Editor Mark Flint (George Bancroft) in Scandal Sheet (1931) prints a story confessing his own crime, the murder of his wife's lover. But he is prompted less by guilt feelings than by his obsession with printing all the news. This same obsession has earlier led him to file a story on his wife's adulterous affair and later, when caught and sentenced, to carry on as editor of the prison paper. Questions of morality rarely influence these heroes.

Even when the reformation is sincere, the films remain cynical. Editor Jerry Strong (Charles Bickford) in Scandal for Sale (1932) discovers he has scruples and abandons the big city for the idyllic innocence of the small town. But he can afford to do so only after he has resorted to some of the most underhanded tactics of the entire cycle in order to win a $25,000 bonus. The best Strong can do is get rich through any means and then leave all the evil behind. The possibility of wider social reform never comes up. Because everyone and everything is corrupt, the reporters' dubious journalism is accepted as quite normal. The films both indulge in the vice through the unrepentant misdeeds of the reporter and condemn it through the reporter's vanquishing of racketeers and debunking of Broadway slickers. Since the targets of the press are all reprehensible, the films avoid confronting the whole issue of moral responsibility.

Only Five Star Final, the best of the cycle along with The Front Page incisively analyzes the implications of the "anything goes" ethic and openly questions a society which requires such compromised principles. It places a subtler perspective on "yellow journalism" by portraying an editor with a conscience and by making the scandalmongers' victims decent people. Randall begins as an idealistic managing editor who tries to run his newspaper in a responsible fashion, printing satires on important social and political issues. But circulation drops and Randall finally admits that "ideals don't put a patch on your pants," bowing to his publisher's demands for more sensational treatments of love nests and murders. He resurrects an old sex murder case which sells more papers but also leads the now happily married, reformed murderess and her husband to commit suicide.

Throughout it all, Randall has been cynically resigned to his scandal-mongering, lightly berating himself and obsessively washing his hands. But when he is ordered to play up the couple's death with another lurid story, he rebels. In a powerfully delivered speech, Randall quits, castigating the publisher for his hypocrisy, for his inhuman, irresponsible manipulation of people's lives for the sake of profit. In Five Star Final, the reporter's amorality is no longer merely a whimsical means of exposing the fradulent but also a dangerous evil in itself capable of destroying the innocent.

Yet righteousness still does not triumph. As Randall walks away from the press building for the last time, the camera focuses on a paper in the gutter. As shouts of "Five Star Final! Read all about it!" blare over the sound track, we are able to distinguish the headline: "Murderess and Husband Commit Suicide." Randall's resignation is an ineffectual gesture which may free him from the corruption but does nothing to arrest the greater evil that grips the city. The only way to survive is to join the rat race and become part of the corruption. Those with scruples are given no alternative but complete withdrawal.

Still, the cycle's portrait of society is not as damning as it could be. Much of the criticism which should be directed against the social system is instead heaped upon a gullible, sensation-hungry public. William Poser (Is My Face Red?) justifies his lurid gossip column, "Keyhole to the City," by claiming he is only giving the public what it wants: "I am a mirror reflecting the spirit of the times," By choosing sensationalism over responsible journalism, the readers are as guilty as the writers who provide the stories. The Secret Six suggests that Scorpio could never exist if there was a public that was vigilant rather than adulatory. Five Star Final, by showing the financial failure of Randall's socially conscious journalism, indicts the readers for the Townsends' tragedy. Randall's comments on the public sum up the press films' attitude: "I could sit on a cigar butt and look down on our readers."

To attack the public for its apathy may be accurate, but the press films never indicate the deeper reasons behind this apathy. It's simply "the spirit of the times" and no connection is made between the failure of society's institutions and the cynicism of its citizens. Throughout the thirties and forties, social unrest was to be seen as the result of an inflammatory and manipulative press acting on a public eager for violence. In this way the films continued to narrow and thereby evade social issues.

Despite its faults, the shyster cycle as a whole communicates an even more severe sense of social breakdown than the fallen woman or convict films. In the frenetic universe of the shyster, everything is a racket. Modern America is an anarchistic circus where free enterprise goes berserk. Richard Griffith accurately captures the overall feel of the shyster cycle: The topical films succeed in voicing a blanket indictment of depression American because their effect was cumulative. It's Tough to be Famous, Love Is a Racket, Beauty for Sale – what wasn't a racket, what couldn't be bought in the third year of the depression? Nothing, answered the topical films, which found a sordid story behind every newspaper headline. Their strength as a movie cycle lay in the fact that the story was really there, and that audiences knew it. "Work and Save," the ancient maxim of individualism, had been succeeded by "Anything Goes." Success in business and love was still the goal of the American wish, but nowadays you get it any way you can.[4]

1. Lewis Milestone on directing The Front Page: "I made them talk even faster than they had in the play; I don't think anybody has made a picture as fast-talking as that." (quoted in Charles Higham and Joel Greenberg, The Celluloid Muse [New York: Signet Books, 1972], p. 177.). Howard Hawks on directing the remake, His Girl Friday (1940): "the characters spoke so fast that the characters kept stepping on each other's lines" (quoted in Andrew Sarris, ed., Interviews with Film Directors [New York: Avon Books, 1970], p. 238.

2. Hecht and MacArthur, The Front Page (New York: Covici-Friede, 1928), p. 40.

3. Ibid., p. 129.

4. Richard Griffith, The Film Till Now (London: Spring Books, 1967), p. 442.

SELECTED FILMOGRAPHY

(* indicates confirmed journalist or former journalist involved in production)

1900

Horsewhipping an Editor
American Mutoscope and Biograph Co.
Editor attacked by irate man for unexplained reason; scrub woman and small boy come to the rescue and rout attacker.

1903

Delivering Newspapers
American Mutoscope & Biograph Co. 27 feet.
A large group of young boys scurries to receive copies of th New York World from a delivery truck in Madison Square, New York.

1910

Gallegher: A Newspaper Story
Edison Company.
From the short story by Richard Harding Davis.*

The Big Scoop
Edison Company.
Discharged reporter regains job with scoop on bank closing.

1911

The Reform Candidate
Edison Company.
Woman reporter exposes collusion between politicians and big utility.

1913

Tapped Wires
Essanay Company. Directed by Theodore Wharton. With: E.H. Calvert, Helen Dunbar.
Rival news agencies try for scoops on train wreck story.

The Grafters
Reliance Company. Directed by Frederick Sullivan. With: Edna Cunningham, Henry Francis Koster.
Reporter foils graft in city street work.

Her Big Story
American Company. With: J. Warren Kerrigan, Charlotte Burton.
Woman reporter exposes corrupt city administration.

1914

The Chechako
Bosworth, Inc. (Paramount). Directed by Hobart Bosworth. Screenplay by Hettie Gray Baker, from the novel Smoke Bellew by Jack London. With: Jack Conway and Myrtle Stedman.*
San Francisco journalist toughens up in the Klondike, wins girl and gold.

Fire and Sword
Kismet Feature Film Co.
Directed by T. Hayes Hunter. With: Isabel Rea and Tom McEvoy.
Reporter rescues a tourist abducted by the Grand Vizier in Tangiers, then marries her.

Power of the Press
Biograph – Klaw & Erlanger. With: Lionel Barrymore, Alan Hale.
Cub reporter vindicates innnocent man and captures counterfeiters.

A Romance of the Mexican Revolution
Copyright Jordan Shenfield, 3 August 1914. (No further information available.)
A young NY reporter sent to Mexico to cover the war uncovers spies and marries the landowner's daughter, giving up his profession.

Trapped in the Great Metropolis
Rolands Feature Film Co. With: Rose Austin.
Woman reporter exposes white slave operation run by fake philanthropist she had previously interviewed.

The Truth Wagon
Masterpiece Film Manufacturing Co. – Alliance Films Corp. Directed by Max Figman. Based on the play by Haydon Talbot. With: Max Figman, Lolita Robertson, H.A. Livingstone.
Wealthy practical joker buys dying newspaper, campaigns against graft, marries former publisher's daughter after fighting off corrupt machine.

The War Extra
Blaché Features.
Ambitious cub reporter in Mexico, suspected of spying by revolutionaries, saved by young Mexican woman whom he brings back to New York in triumph.

1915

The Country Boy
Lasky-Paramount. Directed by Frederick Thomson. Based on the play by Edgar Selwyn. With: Marshal Neilan, Florence Dagmar, Dorothy Green.
New York newspaperman befriends yokel in town and they return to his upstate village to start newspaper, whose success gets yokel his girl.

The Cub
William A. Brady Picture Plays (World Film Corp). Directed by Maurice Tourneur. Based on the Play by Thompson Buchanan.* With: John Hines, Martha Hedman, Robert Cummings.
Reporter sent to cover feud in Kentucky hills falls in love and re-starts feud before all is straightened out.

The Failure
Reliance (Mutual). Written and directed by William Christy Cabanne. With: John Emerson, Wahneta Hanson, A.D. Sears.
Reporter exposes theatrical manager who exploits girls, later writes a play and manager frames him for robbery; escaping prison with his baby dean and wife dying, reporter takes poison and frames manager in turn.

The Galloper
Pathe. Directed by Donald MacKenzie. Screenplay by George Brackett Seitz, from the play by Richard Harding Davis.* With: Clifton Crawford, Melville Stewart and Fania Marinoff.
War correspondent escapes creditors by fleeing to Greece at outbreak of war between Turkey and Greece and is nearly executed for his reporting.

The Gentleman from Indiana
Pallas Pictures – Paramount. Directed by Frank Lloyd. Based on the novel by Booth Tarkington. With: Dustin Farnum, Winifred Kingston, Herbert Standing.
Star athlete buys failing newspaper and uses its crusades as steppingstone to political career; when badly beaten, his girlfriend uses newspaper to expose crooks and engineer his election victory.

The House of Tears
Rolfe Photoplays (Metro Pictures). Directed by Edwin Crane. Screenplay by Frank Dazey. With: Emily Stevens, Henri Bergman, Walter Hitchcock.
Woman reporter unknowingly falls in love with financier who abandoned her mother.

How Molly Malone Made Good
Photo Drama Co. (Kulee Features). Directed by Lawrence B. McGill. Screenplay by Burns Mantle.* With: Marguerite Gale, Helen Hilton, John Reedy.
Immigrant from Ireland proves her abilities and wins reporter's job despite the interference of others on staff.

1916

The Clarion
Equitable M.P. Corp – World Film Corp. Directed by James Durkin. Based on the novel by Samuel Hopkins Adams. With: Carlyle Blackwell, Howard Hall, Marion Dentler.
Quack's son buys newspaper to stop crusade against his father; a new crusade loses him slumlord's daughter as his girlfriend; when anarchists blow up newspaper, all realize the crusades were true and are reconciled.

The Daring of Diana
Vitagraph Co. – V.L.S.E. Directed by S. Rankin Drew. Story by Charles L. Gaskill. With: Anita Stewart, Charles Wellesly, Anders Randolf.
Woman reporter catches crooks and releases publisher's kidnapped father.

The Fourth Estate
Fox. Directed by Frank Powell. Scenario by Frank Powell, based on the play by Joseph Medill Patterson* and Harriet Ford. With: Clifford Bruce, Ruth Blair, Victor Benoit.
Reporter fired by crooked judge after exposing trumped-up charges against strike leader; years later wealthy striker buys paper and hires reporter as managing editor as they together expose judge's crimes.

Half a Rogue
Universal. Directed by Henry Otto. Scenario by Henry Otto, based on the novel by Harold MacGrath. With: King Baggot, Lettie Ford, Clara Beyers.

Newspaper creates scandal in political race in small town, but town doesn't believe newspaper story and elects him.

Her Double Life

Fox Film Corp. Directed by J. Gordon Edwards. Screenplay by Mary Murillo. With: Theda Bara, Stuart Holmes, A.H. Van Buren.

A woman flees to England and takes on false identity to escape the unwanted attentions of a journalist, who turns up at the front and exposes her.

Her Father's Gold

Thanhouser Film Corp. (Mutual). Directed by W. Eugene Moore. Story by Crittenden Mariott. With: Harris Gordon, Barbara Gilroy, William Burt.

Reporter goes to Florida to investigate man-eating alligator, but falls in love and recovers woman's father's stolen gold bullion, with alligator's help.

His Picture in the Papers

Triangle. Directed by John Emerson. Scenario by Anita Loos. With: Douglas Fairbanks.

Doug hungers for success and publicity.

The Little Liar

Fine Arts Film Co. (Triangle). Directed by Lloyd Ingraham. Screenplay by Anita Loos. With: Mae Marsh, Robert Harron, Olga Gray.

Reporter vindicates slum girl from frame-up as shoplifter.

The Lottery Man

F. Ray Comstock Photoplay Corp. – Unity Sales Corp. Based on the play by Rida Johnson Young. With: Thurlow Bergen, Elsie Esmond, Carolyn Lee.

Star athlete turned reporter needing money starts a lottery with himself as prize; when he falls in love he desperately tries to recall all copies of the paper.

The Man From Manhattan

American Film Co. – Mutual. Directed by Jack Halloway. Scenario by James Edward Hungerford. With: William Stowell, Charles Wheelock, Rhea Mitchell.

Modern poet disowned by his father buys small town newspaper, staffs with literati but refuses to endorse crooked politician, who burns down paper and blames editor; vindicated just as town is ready to lynch him, poet/editor is reunited with now proud father.

The Pursuing Vengeance

Unity Pictures Corp. Directed by Martin Sabine. Based on a novel by Burton Egbert Stevenson. With: Sheldon Lewis, Jane Meredity, Henry Mortimer.

Reporter solves puzzling crime involving antique cabinet poisoned by jewel thief.

The Reapers

Triumph Film Corp. (Equitable). Directed by Burton King. Screenplay by Eve Unsell. With: John Mason, Clara Whipple, Joan Morgan.

When publisher is paralyzed in accident, his wife runs off with gambler; unable to work and reduced to selling papers, publisher is healed through faith, and starts evangelizing clubs, where he meets former wife and convinces her to reform at a convent.

The Rummy

Fine Arts Film Co. (Triangle). Directed by Paul Powell. Screenplay by Wilfred Lucas. With: Wilfred Lucas, Pauline Starke, William H. Brown.

Night court reporter marries woman accused of prostitution, later finds her with publisher and becomes a drunk; when he breaks graft story publisher discredited and wife reconciled.

Saving the Family Name

Bluebird Photoplays Inc. Directed by Lois Weber and Phillips Smalley. Scenario by Lois Weber, based on an idea by Evelyn Heath. With: Mary MacLaren, Girrard Alexander, Carl von Schiller.

Newspapers make celebrity of chorus girl involved in love-suicide and she vamps wealthy youngster, but finds herself abducted by his brother on mother's orders; brother realizes her reputation is only engineered by press, but when he tries to return her to his brother, she announces love for abductor.

1917

A Bit of Kindling

Mutual Film Corp. Directed by Sherwood Macdonald. Story by Douglas Bronston. With: Jackie Saunders, Arthur Shirley, J.P. Wade.

Newsgirl fights for her territory, and then defends wealthy young customer from thugs; she runs away from him and years later they are reconciled.

The Food Gamblers

Triangle Film Corp. Directed by Albert Parker. Story by Robert Shirley. With: Wilfred Lucas, Elda Millar, Mac Barnes.

Woman reporter covers food riots in tenements, finds retailers are manipulated by ring of food speculators; when she won't be bribed the head crook falls in love with her and is reformed.

Framing Framers

Triangle Film Corp. Directed by Ferris Hartman or Henri D'Elba. Screenplay by Philip J. Hurn. With: Charles Gunn, Edward Jobson, George Pearce.

Ambitious reporter gets involved in rivalry between two candidates, ultimately forces both corrupt schemers to drop out and wins office himself.

The Hater of Men

NY Motion Picture Corp (Triangle). Directed by Charles Miller. Screenplay by C. Gardner Sullivan. With: Bessie Barriscale, Charles K. French, Jack Gilbert.

Woman reporter disillusioned by marriage while covering sensational divorce, breaks her engagement and turns bohemian, losing friends' respect.

Indiscreet Corinne

Triangle Film Corp. Directed by Jack Dillon. Scenario by George Elwood Jenks. Story by H.B. Daniels. With: Olive Thomas, George Chesebro, Joseph Bennett.

Bored wealthy daughter is hired by newspaper to marry (fake) South American millionaire in publicity stunt, but true love blooms.

The Little Brother

New York Motion Picture Corp. – Triangle. Directed by Charles Miller. Scenario by Lambert Hillyer. Story by Lois Zellner. With: Enid Bennett, William Garwood, Josephine Headley.

To earn her living, girl masquerades as newsboy on streetcorner; chance meeting with benefactor places her in upstate mission school where she becomes a girl again; on graduation she goes to Mexico to join her benefactor, where they marry.

The Night Workers

Essanay. Directed by J. Charles Haydon. Story by J. Bradley Smollen. With: Marguerite Clayton, Jack Gardner, Julien Barton.

Orphan office boy becomes drunken star

reporter and marries colleague to reform by taking post as editor of her grandfather's small-town paper.

Nina, The Flower Girl

Fine Arts Film Co. – Triangle. Directed by Lloyd Ingraham. Scenario by Mary H. O'Connor. With: Bessie Love, Elmer Clifton, Bert Hadley.

Crippled newsboy protects little flower seller, and both are rehabilitated through the generosity of benefactors to live happily ever after.

Out of the Wreck

Oliver Morosco Photoplay Co. – Paramount. Directed by William Desmond Taylor. Scenario by Gardner Hunting. Story by Maude Erve Corsan. With: Kathlyn Williams, William Clifford, William Conklin.

Editor and star reporter digging for scandal on politician's wife during heated election are so moved by her tale that when they find dirt they bury the story.

Over the Hill

Astra Film Corp. – Pathé. Directed by William Parke. Scenario and story by Lois Zellner. With: Gladys Hulette, H.J. Gilmour, Dan Mason.

Minister's daughter takes newspaper job and helps advertising manager prove to owner and his scandalmongering son that yellow journalism is bad for business; ad man is promoted by reformed owner and marries the girl.

Paddy O'Hara

NY Motion Picture Corp/Kay-Bee (Triangle). Directed by Walter Edwards. Screenplay by J. G. Hawks. With: William Desmond, Mary McIvor, Robert McKim.

Star London reporter sent to cover Balkan war falls in love with officer's niece and refuses Foreign Office bribe to annul marriage.

The Penny Philanthropist

Wholesome Films Corp. Directed by Guy McConnell. Based on the novel by Clara E. Laughlin. With: Ralph Morgan, Peggy O'Neil, Frank Wood.

Street newspaper seller gives away a penny a day to the poor, and her millionaire customer asks her to teach him how to give away money.

The Princess of Park Row

Vitagraph Co. Directed by Ashley Miller.

Screenplay by A. Van Buren Powell, from a story by Paul West. With: Mildred Manning, Wallace MacDonald, William Dunn.

Reporter falls in love with princess, thinking her a maid, and breaks story of Ruritanian high-finance shennannegins.

Putting the Bee in Herbert

Edison. Directed by Floyd France. Scenario by Clement D'Art, based on the short story by George Weston. With: Harry Benham, Ethel Fleming, Jessie Stevens.

Impecunious bank clerk gets raises from boss and finds happiness by organizing stunts that get free publicity in newspaper.

The Silence Sellers

Metro Pictures Corp. Directed by Burton L. King. Scenario by Wallace C. Clifton, from a short story by Blair Hall. With: Olga Petrova, Mahlon Hamilton, Wyndham Standing.

Social misunderstandings and manipulations involving a gossip sheet, where the reporter turns out to be a secret service agent and exposes social blackmailer.

Sold at Auction

Balboa Amusement Prod. Co. (Pathe). Directed by Sherwood MacDonald. Screenplay by Daniel Whitcomb. With: Lois Meredith, William Conklin, Marguerite Nichols.

Reporter in love with woman breaks story of white slave auctions just as she is about to be sold to her own father, who had abandoned her.

Truthful Tulliver

New York Motion Picture Corp. – Triangle Distributing. Directed by William S. Hart. Scenario by J.G. Hawks. With: William S. Hart, Nina Byron, Milton Ross.

Frontiersman turned newspaper editor cleans up town and foils corruption to find true love.

The Wild Girl

Eva Tanguay Film Corp. (Selznick Pictures). Directed by Howard Estabrook. Screenplay by George M. Rosener. With: Eva Tanguay, Tom Moore, Stuart Holmes.

Local newspaper editor hires young 'boy' only to find out he is missing heiress abandoned to and raised by gypsies.

1918

Caught in the Act

Fox. Directed by Harry Millarde. Screenplay

by Raymond L. Schrock, from a story by Fred Jackson. With: Peggy Hyland, Leslie Austen, George Bunny.

Reporter who exposed millionaire food profiteer mistakes his daughter for a seamstress, but she plays along and falls in love.

The Empty Cab

Bluebird Photoplays. Directed by Douglas Gerrard. Scenario and story by F. McGrew Willis. With: Franklin Farnum, Eileen Percy, Harry De More.

Cub reporter gets big break by tracking down counterfeiters and releasing kidnapped girl, only to find it is a hoax intended to test his reporter's instincts.

The Floor Below

Goldwyn Pictures Corp. Directed by Clarence G. Badger. Story by Elaine Sterne. With: Mabel Normand, Tom Moore, Helen Dahl.

Prankster copy girl given one last chance and assigned story linking mission with local robberies; she solves crime but abandons job to marry millionaire mission donor.

The Grand Passion

Universal. Directed by Ida May Park. Scenario by Ida May Park, based on a story by Thomas Addison. With: Dorothy Phillips, Jack Mulhall, Lon Chaney.

Corrupt boss of rough-and-tumble western town starts up newspaper to increase his control, but idealistic editor persuades him to reform instead.

His Own Home Town

Famous Players-Lasky Corp. – Paramount. Directed by Victor L. Schertzinger. Scenario by Larry Evans. With: Charles Ray, Katherine MacDonald, Charles K. French.

Struggling playwright is shunned by ministerial father and all others except crusading editor and daughter in corrupt home town; after success under alias in big city he finds editor has willed him paper: he returns to clean up town and marry daughter.

Leap to Fame

World Film Corp. Directed by Carlyle Blackwell. Screenplay by Raymond Schrock. With: Carlyle Blackwell, Evelyn Greeley, Muriel Ostriche.

Judge sends ne'er-do-well son off to NY to work as a reporter, where his first assignment leads to captured spies and kidnapped women, after which he returns home triumphant.

On the Jump
Fox Film Corp. Directed by Raoul A. Walsh. Screenplay by Ralph Spence. Story by Raoul A. Walsh. With: George Walsh, Frances Burnham, James Marcus.

A patriotic reporter resigns when story on Liberty Loans torn up by new publisher; he later reveals publisher as German agent and prevents strike in munitions plant, unmasks spies, and sinks submarine.

Powers That Prey
American Film Co. – Mutual Film Corp. Directed by Henry King. Story by Will M. Ritchey. With: Mary Miles Minter, Alan Forrest, Harvey Clark.

Run out of town for expose, newspaper owner has his daughter take over paper; she redecorates city room and prints fluffy scoops while crooks regroup, but father returns to save the day so she can marry dynamic young editor.

The Ranger
W.H. Clifford Photoplay Co. Directed by Bob Gray. Story by W.H. Clifford. With: Shorty Hamilton, Charles Arling, William Colvin.

Texas Ranger masquerades as reporter to get the goods on editor who is secretly a German spy distributing propaganda across the Mexican border.

Say, Young Fellow!
Famous Players-Lasky Corp. Written and directed by Joseph Henabery. With: Douglas Fairbanks, Marjorie Daw, Frank Campeau.

Cub reporter impresses editor by gaining interview with reluctant financier at gunpoint, then sent to break fraud story and delivers sensational scoop.

Under Suspicion
Universal. Directed by William C. Dowlan. Scenario by Doris Schroeder. Story by Mildred Considine. With: Ora Carew, Forrest Stanley, Frank MacQuarrie.

Newsboy foils plot of imposture and mistaken romance amongst the wealthy.

Unexpected Places
Metro Pictures Corp. Directed by E. Mason Hopper. Screenplay by Albert Shelby Le Vino and George D. Baker, from the novelette by Frank R. Adams. With: Bery Lytell, Rhea Mitchell, Rosemary Theby.

Cub reporter poses as English lord to unmask spies during WW I.

Wanted – A Brother
Oakdale Productions – General Film Co. Directed by Robert Ensminger. Story by L. Virginia Walters. With: Gloria Joy, Mignon LeBrun, H.E. Archer.

Wealthy runaway boy becomes newsboy, framed and convicted by fellow newsboys, is finally shown innocent and reconciled to father by his girl, who had always wanted a brother.

The Way Out
World Film Corp. Directed by George Kelson. Screenplay by Clara S. Beranger, from a story by Jack O'Mara. With: June Elvidge, Carlyle Blackwell, Kate Lester.

Successful journalist is love, but socially ambitious mother foils romance with daughter until last reel.

The Yellow Ticket
Astra Film Corp (Pathe). Directed by William Parke. Screenplay by Tom Cushing, from the play by Michael Morton. With: Fannie Ward, Milton Sills, Warner Oland.

American journalist saves persecuted Russian Jew from discrimination and murder charge.

1919

The Belle of the Season
Metro Pictures Corp. Directed by S. Rankin Drew. Scenario by S. Rankin Drew, inspired by a poem by Ella Wheeler Wilcox. With: Emmy Wehlen, S. Rankin Drew, Walter Hitchcock.

Son of a wealthy newspaper owner works in settlement house and persuades heiress to agree with striking millworkers, whereupon they marry, even though newspaper's story puts him off at end.

The Black Circle
World Film Corp. Directed by Frank Reicher. Scenario by Giles R. Warren. Story by Raymond C. Hill. With: Creighton Hale, Virginia Valli, Jack Drumier.

Male and female New York reporters get fired when they trade assignments and write each other's stories; hired in her home town, they crusade against corruption, rescue her father in election, and marry.

A Fighting Colleen
Vitagraph. Directed by David Smith. Screenplay and story by Gerald C. Duffy. With: Bessie Love, Ann Schaefer, Charles Spere.
Spunky Irish girl supports mother by selling newspapers, then helps district attorney break mayor's tenement graft ring.

Ginger
World Film Corp. Directed by Burton George. Scenario by Raymond L. Schrock. Story by Burton George. With: Violet Palmer, Raymond Hackett, Paul Everton.
Abused girl befriended by newsboy; when her father is convicted she is adopted by the judge and becomes interested in his son; years later the boys meet in the battle of Chateau Thierry, and the newsboy dies in the arms of his girl, now a nurse, whereupon she marries the judge's son.

The Grim Game
Famous Players-Lasky Corp. Directed by Irvin Willat. Screenplay by Walter Woods. Story by Arthur B. Reeve and John W. Grey. With: Harry Houdini, Thomas Jefferson, Ann Forrest.
Reporter (Houdini) plants evidence implicating him in the fake murder of his girlfriend's uncle for story about circumstantial evidence; when uncle is killed, he has a series of remarkable escapes to catch real killer.

The Haunted Bedroom
Thomas H. Ince Prod. (Famous Players-Lasky). Directed by Fred Niblo. Screenplay and story by C. Gardner Sullivan. With: Enid Bennett, Dorcas Matthews, Jack Nelson.
Woman reporter catches international forger who is haunting estate in Virginia.

I'll Get Him Yet
New Art Film Co. (Famous Players-Lasky). Directed by Elmer Clifton. Story by Harry Carr. With: Dorothy Gish, George Fawcett, Richard Barthelmess.
Reporter pursued by traction trust millionaire's daughter learns to give up protesting trolley service and live with money.

The Lost Princess
Fox. Directed by Scott Dunlap. Scenario by Scott Dunlap. Story by J. Anthony Roack. With: Albert Ray, Elinor Fair, George Hernandez.
Farmboy studies journalism by correspondence, but in the city he cannot find work until recommended by a sob sister; when her boyfriend tries to ruin his career she helps him concoct a romantic adventure feature: they marry even though he wakes to find it all a dream.

The Lottery Man
Famous Players-Lasky Corp. – Paramount/Artcraft. Directed by James Cruze. Scenario by Elmer Harris, adapted by Frank Urson from the play by Rida Johnson Young. With: Wallace Reid, Harrison Ford, Wanda Hawley.
Broke reporter loses loan in stock market, then dreams up promotion lottery with himself as groom for prize; unable to cancel the lottery when he falls in love, is saved by winning maid who marries butler, leaving him free. (Remake of 1916 title.)

The Microbe
Metro Pictures Corp. Directed by Henry Otto. Screenplay by June Mathis, based on the short story by Henry Altimus. With: Viola Dana, Kenneth Harlan, Arthur Maude.
Girl newspaper seller dresses as boy to avoid harassment, and becomes protege/literary inspiration of wealthy author, who finally marries her.

Todd of the Times
Robert Brunton Co. – Pathé. Directed by Eliot Howe. Scenario by Jack Cunningham. Story by Jack Cunningham and John Lynch. With: Frank Keenan, Buddy Post, Aggie Herring.
Newshound city editor too shy to become managing editor and severely henpecked at home, until he breaks up gambling ring in town with crusading story, gets promotion, and breaks domination of wife at home.

The Mystery of the Yellow Room
Mayflower Photoplay Corp (Realart). Written and directed by Emile Chautard. Based on the novel by Gaston Leroux. With: William S. Walcott, Edmund Elton, George Cowl. Reporter solves locked-room murder that baffles police.

The Woman Under Cover
Universal. Directed by George Seigmann. Screenplay by Harvey Thew, from a play by Sada Cowan. With: Fritzi Brunette, George McDaniel, Harry Springler.
Woman reporter breaks story of her brother's wife's murder of a Broadway star, then resigns to marry editor and help brother.

1920

Deadline at Eleven

Vitagraph. Directed by George Fawcett. Scenario by Lucien Hubbard. Story by Ruth Byers. With: Corinne Griffith, Frank Thomas, Webster Campbell.

Socialite gets job on newspaper, to much derision, but becomes sob sister and saves inebriate reporter/beau by solving murder case, whereupon he reforms and they marry.

Dinty

Associated First National. Directed by Marshall Neilan and John McDermott. Scenario by Marion Fairfax. Story by Marshall Neilan. With: Wesley Barry, Colleen Moore, Tom Gallery.

Newsboy supports sick mother, cracks opium smuggling ring in Chinatown and, when mother dies, is adopted by judge to start life anew.

The Fear Market

Realart Pictures Corp. Directed by Kenneth Webb. Scenario by Clara Beranger, based on the play by Amélie Rives. With: Alice Brady, Frank Losee, Harry Mortimer.

Socialite daughter teams up with crusading publisher to sink scandal sheet, unaware her father is the secret owner; when revealed, father reforms and couple marry.

The Fourth Face

Fidelity Pictures. Story by Marjorie Van Beuran.

Woman reporter solves murder of woman in deserted mansion. (Note: possibly The Invisible Web, Fidelity, 1921, dir Beverly C. Rule, or The Mystery of Washington Square, Fidelity, 1920)

Go and Get It

First National. Directed by Marshall Neilan and Henry Symonds. Story by Marion Fairfax. With: Pat O'Malley, Wesley Barry, Agnes Ayres.

Publisher conspires with rival to wreck his own paper and take over ownership, but woman owner takes job at paper in disguise and, helped by star reporter, uncovers the truth and solves murders, whereupon they marry.

The Green Flame

Robert Brunton Prod. (W.W. Hodkinson/ Pathe). Directed by Ernest C. Warde. Screenplay by Jack Cinningham. Story by Raymond G. Hill. With: J. Warren Kerrigan, Fritzi Brunette, Jay Morley.

Woman reporter and boyfriend foil jewel thieves.

The Heart of Twenty

Brentwood Film Corp (Robertson-Cole). Directed by Henry Kolker. Story by Sarah Y. Mason. With: ZaSu Pitts, Jack Pratt, Percy Challenger.

Undercover reporter breaks up auto theft ring.

Homespun Folks

Thomas H. Ince productions (Associated Producers). Directed by John Griffith Wray. Screenplay by Julien Josephson*. With: Lloyd Hughes, Gladys George, George Webb.

Lawyer turned out of home by his father falls in love with editor's daughter and saves her father from politically motivated charge of murder.

In the Heart of a Fool

Mayflower Photoplay Corp. Directed by Alan Dwan. Screenplay by Lillian Ducey, from the novel by William Allen White.* With: James Kirkwood, Anna Q. Nilsson, Mary Thurman.

Socialite teases journalist beau with another man; heartbroken, he takes up with vamp and they are reconciled only years later.

The Jailbird

Thomas H. Ince Productions - Famous Players- Lasky/Paramount. Directed by Lloyd Ingraham. Scenario and story by Julien Josephson*. With: Douglas MacLean, Doris May, Lew Morrison.

Jailbird and prison printer inherit small town western newspaper, and set up land scam, but just as they leave town oil is struck on the land, and jailbird marries society editor, deciding his destiny is to be an honest man.

The Little Wanderer

Fox. Directed by Howard M. Mitchell. Scenario and story by Denison Clift. With: Shirley Mason, Raymond McKee, Cecil Vanauker.

Son of publisher accuses father of exploiting the poor to increase circulation, then goes to work on skid row, falls in love with disguised woman, who is revealed as daughter of publisher's crooked former partner, but her father reappears to reveal publisher was real crook.

The Money-Changers

Federal Photoplay, Inc. (Pathe). Directed by Jack Conway. Screenplay by William H. Clifford. Story by Benjamin B. Hampton and Upton Sinclair, from the novel by Sinclair. With: Robert McKim, Claire Adams, Roy Stewart.

Reporter wins love of settlement house proprietress while exposing white slave and drug rings in Chinese district.

The Silent Barrier

Louis Tracy Prod. (W.W. Hodkinson/Pathe). Directed by William Worthington. Screenplay by Charles T. Dazy, from the novel by Louis Tracy. With: Sheldon Lewis, Corinne Barker, Florence Dixon.

Woman society reporter reconciles father and daughter after adventures in the Swiss Alps.

Whispers

Selznick Pictures Corp. (Select). Directed by William P.S. Earle. Screenplay by George D. Proctor. Story by Marc Connelly. With: Elaine Hammerstein, Matt Moore, Phillips Tead.

Scandal sheet reporter unwittingly falls in love with woman in story, and resigns paper to marry when her identity is revealed.

1921

The Passionate Pilgrim

Cosmopolitan Pictures. Directed by Robert G. Vignola. Scenario by Donald Darrell and George Dubois Proctor, from a novel by Samuel Merwin. With: Matt Moore, Mary Newcome, Marjory Daw.

Reporter exposes crooks to win sob sister.

A Certain Rich Man

Great Authors Pictures. Directed by Howard Hickman. From the novel by William Allen White. *With: Carl Gantvoort, Claire Adams.*

Young banker saved from shortage by new newspaper in small town; years later he is power and publisher is drunk, but at end banker repents and distributes fortune.

Don't Neglect Your Wife

Goldwyn. Directed by Wallace Worsley. Scenario by Louis Sherwin from a story by Gertrude Franklin Atherton. With: Mabel Julienne Scott, Lewis S. Stone, Charles Clary.

1876: reporter turns to alcoholism after falling in love with married socialite, then is redeemed.

The Magic Cup

Realart Pictures. Directed by John S. Robertson. Scenario and story by E. Lloyd Sheldon. *With: Constance Binney, Vincent Coleman, Blanche Craig.*

Cub reporter foils crooks by showing hotel maid is lost aristocrat.

The Secret of the Hills

Vitagraph. Directed by Chester Bennett. Scenario by E. Magnus Ingleton from a novel by William Garrett. With: Antoinio Moreno, Lillian Hall, Kingsley Benedict.

American reporter in London on trail of royal treasure and a girl.

The Family Closet

Playgoers Pictures. Directed by John B. O'Brien. From a story by Will J. Payne. With: Holmes Herbert, Alice Mann, Kempton Greene.

Editor uses newspaper to flush out crook, then blackmails him.

Red Courage

Universal. Directed by Reeves Eason. Scenario by Harvey Gates *from a book by Peter Bernard Kyne. With: Hoot Gibson, Joel Day, Molly McCormick.*

Newspaper in western small town starts reform campaign.

The Star Reporter

Arrow Film Corp. Directed by Duke Worne. From a novel by Wyndham Martin. With: Billie Rhodes, Truman Van Dyke, William Horne.

Reporter hides identity, then gets promotion to editor with scoop on kidnapping.

1922

The Man Under Cover

Universal. Directed by Tod Browning. Scenario by Harvey Gates *from a story by Louis Victor Eytinge. With: Herbert Rawlinson, George Hernandex, William Courtwright.*

Swindler reforms by buying newspaper and conning former partners.

Smudge

First National Exhibitor's Circuit. Directed by Charles Ray. Story and scenario by Rob Wagner. Titles by Edward Withers. With: Charles Ray, Charles K. French, Florence Oberle.

Publisher's son uses newspaper to fight smudge pots in orange groves; when rival politicians and father fight him, he unveils new invention and wins.

The Unfoldment

Producer's Pictures. Directed by George Kern and Murdock MacQuarrie. Story and scenario by James Couldwell and Reed Heustis. With: Florence Lawrence, Barbara Bedford, Charles French.

Love and political scandal complicate life for male and female reporters when editor's attention turns from paper to playmates.

The Woman's Side

Associated First National. Directed by J. A. Barry. Written by J. A. Barry. Scenario by Elliott Clawson.* Produced by B.P. Schulberg.* With: Katherine MacDonald, Edward Burns, Henry Barrows.

Daughter of candidate for governor unmasks smear to rival candidate when she falls in love with newspaper publisher's son.

The Cub Reporter

Goldstone Pictures. Directed by Jack Dillon. Scenario by George Elwood Jenks. With: Richard Talmadge, Jean Calhoun, Edwin B. Tilton.

Reporter braves perils of Chinese underworld to recover sacred jewel.

Extra! Extra!

Fox. Directed by William K. Howard. Scenario by Arthur J. Zellner, from a story by Julien Josephson*. With: Edna Murphy, Johnnie Walker, Hershcel Mayall.

Reporter uses disguises and acting abilities to get stories and solve crime.

Living Lies

Mayflower Pictures. Directed by Emile Chautard. From a story and novel by Arthur Somers Roche.* With: Edmund Lowe, Mona Kingsley, Kenneth Hill.

Reporter uncovers and breaks traction scandal.

The Lying Truth

American Reliance. Direction, story, and scenario by Marion Fairfax. With: Noah Beery, Marjorie Daw, Tully Marshall.

Murder Hoax leads to inheritance in newspaper family.

Front Page Story

Vitagraph. Directed by Jesse Robbins. Scenario by F.W. Beebe. Story by Arthur Frederick Goodrich. With: Edward Everett Horton, Lloyd Ingraham, James Corrigan.

Reporter gets job through bluff, then reconciles editor and mayor.

1923

The Day of Faith

Goldwyn. Directed by Tod Browning. Adaptation by June Mathis and Katharine Kavanaugh, from a book by Arthur Somers Roche.* With: Eleanor Boardman, Tyrone Power, Raymond Griffith.

Reporter hired to expose mission instead volunteers and supports its good works.

Her Reputation

First National Pictures. Directed by John Griffith Wray. Supervised by Thomas Ince. Scenario by Bradley King. With: May McAvoy, Lloyd Hughes, James Corrigan.

Reporter vindicates girl, marries her, and kills competitor's story.

Legally Dead

Universal. Directed by William Parke. Scenario by Harvey Gates* from a story by Charles Furthman. With: Milton Sills, Margaret Campbell, Claire Adams.

Reporter on death row to prove theory that most condemned men are innnocent; on parole he thwarts robbery but is thought a crook and convicted of policeman's murder; innocence discovered too late, he is executed and declared legally dean, but doctor revives him with adrenalin.

Playing It Wild

Vitagraph. Directed by William Duncan. Story and scenario by C. Graham Baker. With: William Duncan, Edith Johnson, Francis Powers.

Robbery ruse of western newspaper elects honest new sheriff.

The Printer's Devil

Warner Brothers. Directed by William Beaudine. Story and scenario by Julien Josephson*. With: Wesley Barry, Harry Myers, Kathryn McGuire.

Small-town newspaperman solves crime and gets girl.

Sinner or Saint

Selznick Distributing Corp. Directed by Lawrence Windom. Scenario by Dorothy Farnum from a story by Dorothy Farnum. With: Betty Blythe, William P. Carleton, Gypsy O'Brien.

Fortune-teller exposed in newspaper stories.

The Steadfast Heart

Goldwyn-Cosmopolitan Corp. Directed by Sheridan Hall. Adaptation by Philip Lonergan

from a novel by Clarence Buddington Kelland. * *With: Marguerite Courtot, Miriam Batista, Joseph Striker.*
Crook turns newspaperman and saves town.

The Town Scandal
Universal. Directed by King Baggot. Scenario by Hugh Hoffman from a novel by Frederick Arnold Kummer. With: Gladys Walton, Edward Hearne, Edward McWade.
Small-town purity league gives up blue laws after Broadway chorine and reporter publish her story of 'friends' in New York.

The Wild Party
Universal. Directed by Herbert Blache. Screenplay by Hugh Hoffman, from a story by Marion Orth. With: Gladys Walton, Robert Ellis, Freeman Wood.
Editor's secretary's society story causes libel suit, but her efforts to prove facts lead to marriage with plaintiff.

1924

The Average Woman
C.C. Burr Pictures. Directed by William 'Christy' Cabanne. Scenario by Raymond S. Harris, from a story by Dorothy de Jagers. With: Pauline Garon, David Powerll, Harrison Ford.
Reporter's story on average woman leads to marriage.

Dynamite Smith
Pathe. Directed by Ralph Ince. Story and scenario by C. Gardner Sullivan. With: Charles Ray, Jacqueline Logan, Bessie Love, Wallace Beery.
Timid San Francisco reporter assigned to murder case runs off with killer's wife; followed to Alaska, he finally captures the crook in a bear trap.

The Fatal Mistake
Perfection Pictures. Directed by Scott Dunlap. With: William Fairbanks, Eva Novak, Wilfred Lucas.
Cub reporter's featured story and photo on socialite are fake, so he loses job until he gets the real story and solves her jewel robbery.

The Flaming Crisis
Merco Productions. Produced by Lawrence Goldman. With: Calvin Nicholson, Dorothy Dunbar.
Young Negro reporter convicted of murder on circumstantial evidence; escapes and goes West where he falls for cowgirl, captures

bandits, and reveals identity to find real murderer has confessed.

Hold Your Breath
Christie. Directed by Scott Sidney. Story by Frank Roland Conklin. With: Dorothy Devore, Walter Hiers, Tully Marshall.
When brother loses reporter job, sister takes it and muffs stories, finally chasing monkey with jewelry up a skyscraper.

The Humming Bird
Paramount. Directed by Sidney Olcott. Adaptation by Forrest Halsey * from a play by Maude Fulton. With: Gloria Swanson, Edward Burns, William Ricciardi.*
Woman Apache dancer loves American reporter in Paris who enlists and is wounded; they are reunited when she escapes jail to be with him.

Hutch of the U.S.A.
New California Film Corp. Directed by James Chapin. Story and scenario by J.F. Natteford. * *With: Charles Hutchinson, Edith Thornton, Frank Leigh.*
American reporter on assignment in banana republic aids revolutionaries, who are defeated by government.

Midnight Secrets
Rayart Pictures. Directed by Jack Nelson. With: George Larkin, Ollie Kirby, Pauline Curley.
Crooks kidnap reporter's girl in hopes of stopping exposé but are captured by paper.

The Pell Street Mystery
Rayart Pictures. Directed by Joseph Franz. With: Georg Larkin, Carl Silvera.
Reporter solves murder in Chinatown.

The Whispered Name
Universal. Directed by King Baggot. Scenario by Lois Zellner, from a play by Rita Weiman and Alice Leal Pollock. With: Ruth Clifford, Charles Clary, William E. Lawrence.
Woman reporter on social beat discovers plot to sue her to socialite can get divorce, but news editor saves the day.

1925

Contraband
Paramount. Directed by Alan Crosland. Screenplay by Jack Cunningham from a novel by Clarence Buddington Kelland. * *With: Lois Wilson, Noah Beery, Raymond Hatton.*
Woman publisher in small town leads campaign against bootleggers, cleans up town.

The Devil's Cargo
Paramount. Directed by Victor Fleming. Screenplay by A.P. Younger. Story by Charles E. Whittaker. With: Wallace Beery, Pauline Starke, Claire Adams.
Action picture set around an 1849 Gold Rush newspaper.

The Fighting Cub
Truart Film Corp. Directed by Paul Hurst. Story by Adele Buffington. With: Wesley Barry, Mildred Harris, Pat O'Malley.
Cub becomes reporter by reforming philanthropist from crime.

Headlines
Directed by E.H. Griffith. Screenplay by Peter Milne. With: Alice Joyce, Malcolm McGregor, Virginia Lee Corbin.
Feature writer protects secret daughter, who marries editor after scandal breaks.

How Baxter Butted In
Warner Brothers. Directed by William Beaudine. Scenario by Owen Davis. Adaptation by Julien Josephson★, from a story by Harold Titus. With: Dorothy Devore, Matt Moore, Ward Crand.
Shy circulation clerk finds happiness.

The Last Edition
FBO. Directed by Emory Johnson. Story and scenario by Emilie Johnson. With: Ralph Lewis, Lita Leslie, Ray Hallor.
Composing room foreman, reporter, and girl break political scandal. Interiors used the San Francisco Chronicle plant.

A Man Must Live
Paramount. Directed by Paul Sloane. Scenario by James Ashmore Creelman, from a story by Ida Alexa Ross Wylie. With: Richard Dix, Jacqueline Logan, George Nash.
Reporter with principles on New York scandal sheet in conflict with editor over stories that ruin lives; assaults editor and loses job but wins lawsuit against steel company.

My Lady's Lips
B.P. Schulberg Productions. Directed by James P. Hogan. Story and continuity by John Goodrich. With: Alyce Mills, William Powell, Clara Bow.
Star reporter poses as crook to expose gambler and save editor's daughter.

The Part Time Wife
Lumas. Directed by Henry McCarty.★ Scenario by Victoria Moore and Henry McCarty.

Adaptation by James J. Tyman from a story by Peggy Gaddis. Produced by Sam Sax. With: Alice Calhoun, Robert Ellis, Freeman Wood.
Film star marries poor reporter, and difficulties ensue until his play is a success.

Salome of the Tenements
Paramount. Directed by Sidney Olcott. Scenario by Sonya Levien,★ from a novel by Angia Yezierska.
Jewish woman reporter marries millionaire, is blackmailed by moneylender and wins. (set on Hester Street)

Youth and Adventure
FBO. Directed by James W. Horne. Story and continuity by Frank Howard Clark. With: Richard Talmadge, Peter Gordon, Joseph Girard.
Comedy of wastrel installed as city editor by gangster to keep him silent, but editor uses crook's own paper to expose his racket.

1926

Atta Boy
Pathe. Directed by Edward H. Griffith. Story and continuity by Charles Horan, Alf Goulding. Titles by Harold Christie. With: Monty Banks, Virginia Bradford, Ernie Wood.
As practical joke, copy boy is told he is a reporter; writes story on fake kidnapping that turns out to be real; solves crime, gets scoop and reward.

Dangerous Traffic
Goodwill Pictures. Directed by Bennett Cohn. Written by Bennett Cohn. With: Francix X. Bushman, Jack Perrin, Mildred Harris.
Seaside reporter breaks up smuggling ring.

The Hollywood Reporter
Hercules Productions. Directed by Bruce Mitchell. Story and scenario by Grover Jones. With: Frank Merrill, Charles K. French, Peggy Montgomery.
Reporter wins editor's daughter by exposing boss in city.

Is That Nice?
FBO. Directed by Del Andrews. Adaptation and continuity by Paul Gangelin. Story by Walter A. Sinclair. With: George O'Hara, Doris Hill, Stanton Heck.
Cub reporter breaks political scandal, wins girl.

Lightning Reporter
Elbee Pictures. Directed by Jack Noble. Scenario by Jack Noble. Story by Tom Gibson.

With: Johnny Walker, Sylvia Breamer, Barry McIntosh.
Cub reporter helps railroad magnate best competition in stock market, wins daughter.

Looking for Trouble
Universal. Directed by Robert North Bradbury. Scenario by George C. Hinely. Story by Stephen Chalmers. With: Jack Hoxie, Marcelline Day, J. Gordon Russell.
Small western newspaper catches diamond smugglers.

Man Rustlin'
FBO. Directed by Del Andrews. Story by William Branch. Continuity by Burl R. Tuttle and Jay Chapman. With: Bob Custer, Florence Lee, Jules Cowles.
Western reporter on small paper catches bandits and is so successful he becomes syndicated columnist on big Eastern paper.

The Man Upstairs
Warner Brothers. Directed by Roy Del Ruth. *
Screenplay by Edmund T. Lowe, Jr., from a story by Earl Derr Biggers. With: Monte Blue, Dorothy Devore, Helen Dunbar.
Love story starts in personals column of newspaper.

Man, Woman and Sin
MGM. Directed by Monta Bell. Scenario by Alice D.G. Miller. Titles by John Coulton. With: John Gilbert, Jeanne Eagles, Gladys Brockwell.
Reporter loves society editor, who dates publisher; murder, perjury, reconciliation.

Oh, What a Nurse
Warner Brothers. Directed by Charles Reisner. Adaptation by Darryl Francis Zanuck from a play by Robert Emmett Sherwood and Bertroam Bloch. With: Sydney Chaplin, Patsy Ruth Miller, Gayne Whitman.*
Reporter subs lovelorn columnist and gets involved in society marriage, crooks.

Out of the Storm
Tiffany. Directed by Louis Gasnier. Scenario by Lois Hutchinson, Leete Renick Brown, from a story by Arthur Stringer. With: Jacqueline Logan, Tyrone Power, Edmund Burns.
Publisher's son kept from murder charge by indomitable editor.

Rainbow Riley
First National. Directed by Charles Hines. Titles by John W. Krafft, from a play by Thompson Buchanan (The Cub). With: Johnny Hines, Brenda Bond, Bradley Barker.*

Reporter chased by both sides of Kentucky feud.

The Social Highwayman
Warner Brothers. Directed by William Beaudine. Adaptation by Edward T. Lowe, Jr, and Philip Klein, from a story by Darryl Francis Zanuck. With: John Patrick, Dorothy Devore, Montagu Love.
Cub reporter sent to investigate bandit is held up, then ridiculed by colleagues and rival papers who send him out again to capture crook.

Stepping Along
Directed by Charles Hines. From a story by Matt Taylor. With: Mary Brian, Johnny Hines, William Gaxton.
City Hall newsboy dreams of actress and politics; achieves both after defeating crooks.

Stick to Your Story
Rayart. Directed by Harry J. Brown. Scenario by Henry Roberts Symonds. Titles by Arthur Q. Hagerman. Story by Ralph O. Murphy. With: Billy Sullivan, Estelle Bradley, Melbourne MacDowell.
Cub reporter has weakness for passing up assignments for stories he thinks are better.

1927
A Bowery Cinderella
Excellent Pictures. Directed by Burton King. Scenario by Adrian Johnson. Titles by Harry Chandlee. With: Gladys Hulette, Pat O'Malley, Kate Bruce.
Reporter's girl involved with rich backer until reporter's play succeeds.

The Final Extra
Gotham Pictures. Directed by James P. Hogan. Story and scenario by Herbert C. Clark. With: Marguerite de la Motte, Grant Withers, John Miljan.
Young columnist aspires to colleague's crime story; jails bootleggers when his own theatrical impresario is revealed as gang leader.

Grinning Guns
Universal. Directed by Albert Gogell. Story and scenario by Grover Jones. With: Jack Hoxie, Ena Gregory, Robert Milasch.
Western newspaper reforms town. A Blue-Streak Western.

Not for Publication
FBO. Directed by Ralph Ince. Scenario by

Ewart Adamson, from a story by Robert Welles Ritchie. Produced by Joseph P. Kennedy. With: Ralph Ince, Ray Laidlaw, Rex Lesse.
Editor sends reporter to burglarize safe of dam construction agent, then makes own deal with contractor before dam is blown up.

The Secret Studio
Fox. Directed by Victor Schertzinger. Scenario by James Kevin McGuinness★ from the novel by Hazel Livingston (serialized in the San Francisco Call). With: Olive Borden, Clifford Holland, Noreen Philips.
Woman disgraced as newspapers print that she posed for artist in the nude.

1928
The Big Noise
First National. Directed by Alan Dwan. Adaptation and scenario by Tom J. Geraghty. Titles by George Marion, Jr. Story by Ben Hecht.★ With: Chester Conklin, Alice White.
Newspaper exaggerates man's injury to promote subway reform, elects candidate, then ignores injured man.

Broken Barriers
Excellent Pictures. Directed by Burton King. Scenario and titles by Isadore Bernstein. Story by Caroline F. Hayward. With: Helene Costello, Gaston Glass, Joseph Girard.
Reporter gets story on boss killing candidate, but editor holds story when reporter and boss's daughter marry.

Crooks Can't Win
RKO. Directed by George M. Arthur. Story by Joseph Jefferson O'Neill. Adaptation by Enid Hibbard. Titles by Randolph Bartlett.★ With: Ralph Lewis, Thelma Hill, Sam Nelson.
Reporter clears innocent cop suspected of complicity with silk thieves.

Deliverance
Stanley Advertising Co. Directed by B. K. Blake. Scenario by Duncan Underhill, from two books by Irving Fisher.
Washington politics on prohibition bill involves reporters and lobbyists.

Freedom of the Press
Universal. Directed by George Melford. Adaptation and continuity by J. Grubb Alexander. Titles by Walter Anthony. Story by Peter B. Kyne. With: Lewis Stone, Marceline Day, Henry B. Walthall.
Crusading reporter keeps crook from becoming mayor.

Hot News
Paramount. Directed by Clarence Badger. Scenario by Florence Ryerson. Story by Monte Brice and Harlan Thompson.★ With: Bebe Daniels, Neil Hamilton, Paul Lukas.
Newsreel camerawoman finds happiness with Scoop Morgan.

Jazzland
Quality Distributors. Directed by Dallas M. Fitzgerald. Scenario by Ada McQuillan. Titles by Tom Miranda. Story by Samuel Merwin. With: Bryant Washburn, Vera Reynolds, Carrol Nye.
Reporter exposes crooks behind big-city nightclub invading small New England town.

Let 'Er Go Gallegher
Pathe. Directed by Elmer Clifton. Adaptation and continuity by Elliot Clawson.★ Titles by John Krafft.★ Based on series of stories by Richard Harding Davis.★ With: Junior Coghlan, Harrison Ford, Elinor Fair.
Newsboy and reporter solve crimes.

Lightning Speed
FBO. Directed by Robert North Bradbury. Story and continuity by Robert North Bradbury. Titles by Randolph Bartlett.★ With: Bob Steele, Mary Maybery, Perry Murdock.
Reporter thwarts kidnap of governor's daughter by crook seeking pardon of his brother.

Out With the Tide
Peerless. Directed by Charles Hutchinson. Scenario by Elaine Towne. Titles by Paul Perez. Story by John C. Brownell and C. Marion Burton. With: Dorothy Dwan, Cullen Landis, Crawford Kent.
Reporter suspected of murder finds real killer by trailing him to Shanghai.

The Power of the Press
Columbia. Directed by Frank Capra. Adaptation and continuity by Frederick A. Thompson and Sonya Levien.★ Story by Frederick A. Thompson. With: Douglas Fairbanks, Jr., Jobyna Ralston, Mildren Harris.
Cub reporter breaks political scandal and solves crime, gets girl.

Riders of the Dark
MGM. Directed by Nick Grinde. Story and continuity by W.S. van Dyke. Titles by Madeline Ruthven. With: Tim McCoy, Dorothy Dwan, Rex Lease.
Western newspaper is destroyed after start-

ing reform campaign.

Show Girl

First National. Directed by Alfred Santell. Scenario by James T. O'Donoghue. Titles by George Marion. From a novel by Joseph Patrick McEvoy. With: Alice White, Donald Reed, Lee Moran.

Cynical reporter persuades girl involved in nightclub murder to hide out so he can build kidnapping story.

Telling the World

MGM. Directed by Sam Wood. Scenario by Raymond L. Schrock. Titles by Joe Farnham. Story by Dale van Avery. With: William Haines, Anita Page, Elieen Percy.*

Disowned son becomes reporter, catches murderer, saves chorus girl in China.

What a Night!

Paramount. Directed by Edward Sutherland. Screenplay by Louise Long. Titles by Herman J. Mankiewicz. Story by Grover Jones and Lloyd Corrigan. With: Bebe Daniels, Neil Hamilton, William Austin.*

Industrialist's daughter works on newspaper and breaks up political gang.

A Woman Against the World

Tiffany. Directed by George Archaimbaud. Continuity by Gertrude Orr. Titles by Frederic Harron and Fanny Hatton. Story by Albert Shelby Le Vine. With: Harrison Ford, Georgia Hale, Lee Moran.

Girl reporter loves condemned man and proves him innocent in face of editor's antagonism.

1929

Big News

Pathe. Directed by Gregory La Cava. Screenplay by Walter de Leon. Dialogue by Frank Reicher. Adaptation by Jack Jungmeyer. Story by George Brooks. With: Robert Armstrong, Carole Lombard.

Fired reporter investigates dope ring headed by publisher's friend, gets job and wife back with scoop.

Drag

National. Directed by Frank Lloyd. Screenplay by Gene Towne. Dialogue and adaptation by Bradley King, from a book by William Dudley Pelley. With: Richard Barthelmess, Lucien Littlefield.

Reporter on small Vermont newspaper turns playwright, then set designer, for movies in Hollywood.

Gentlemen of the Press

Paramount. Directed by Millard Webb. Screenplay by Bartlett Cormack, from a play by Ward Morehouse. With: Walter Huston, Katherine Francis, Charles Ruggles.*

Star reporter's dedication to job keeps him from reaching own daughter, who dies in childbirth as big story breaks.

Idaho Red

FBO. Directed by Robert de Lacey. Story and continuity by Frank Howard Clark. Titles by Helen Gregg. With: Tom Tyler, Patricia Caron, Frankie Darro.

Orphaned newsboy helps guardian outwit western counterfeiters.

In the Headlines

Warner Brothers. Directed by John G. Adolfi. Screenplay by Joseph Jackson. Story by James A. Starr. With: Grant Withers, Marion Nixon, Clyde Cook.*

Star reporter and woman cub solve double murder.

The Lure of the Atlantic

(GB) H. B. Parkinson (Fox). Written and directed by Norman Lee. With: Eric Hales and Iris Derbyshire.

While Alcock & Brown fly the Atlantic, a reporter is robbed and a broke gambler wins bet.

The Office Scandal

Pathe. Directed by Paul Stein. Original story and adaptation by Paul Gangelin and Jack Jungmeyer. Titles by John Krafft. With: Phyllis Haver, Lesie Fenton, Raymond Hatton.*

Sob sister keeps reporter boyfriend from jail by nailing crooks.

Protection

Fox. Directed by Benjamin Stoloff. Scenario by Frederick Hazlett Brennan. Story by J. Clarkson Miller. With: Robert Elliott, Pal Page, Dorothy Burgess.

Bootlegging story leads to politics, as reporter moves from big paper to independent so he can print truth.

Red Hot Speed

Universal. Directed by Joseph Henabery. Scenario by Gladys Lehman and Matt Taylor. Titles by Albert de Mord. Story by Gladys Lehman. Adaptation by Faith Thomas. With: Reginald Denny, Alice Day, Charles Byer.

Publisher's daughter arrested in midst of newspaper anti-speeding campaign.

Speakeasy

Fox. Directed by Benjamin Stoloff. Scenario by Frederick Hazlitt Brennan and Edwin Burke. Dialogue by Edwin Burke. From a play by Edward Knoblock and George Rosener.* With: Lola Lane, Stuart Erwin, Paul Page.

Woman reporter falls for boxing champ and proves his manager is crooked.

1930

Conspiracy

RKO. Directed by Christy Cabanne. Screenplay and dialogue by Beulah Marie Dix. Produced by William Le Baron.* From a book by Robert Melville Baker and John Emerson.* With: Bessie Love, Ned Sparks, Hugh Trevor.

Reporter helps solve murder and break narcotics ring.

The Czar of Broadway

Universal. Directed by William James Craft. Story, continuity, and dialogue by Gene Towne. With: John Wray, Betty Compson, John Harry.

Based on the life of Arthur Rothstein.

The Divorce

MGM. Directed by Robert Z. Leonard. Continuity and dialogue by John Meehan. Treatment by Nick Grinde and Zelda Sears from a novel by Katharine Ursula Parrott. With: Norma Shearer, Chester Morris, Conrad Nagle.

Marital adventures and crises of reporter and wife.

Loose Ends

(GB) BIP (Wardour) Screenplay by Dion Titheradge and Norman Walker. With: Edma Best and Owen Nares.

Girl reporter blackmailed for learning that man is freed murderer.

Night Ride

Universal. Directed by John S. Robertson. Adaptation by Edward T. Lowe, Jr., from a story by Henry LaCossitt. Titles by Charles Logue.* Dialogue by Tom Reed* and Edward T. Logue, Jr. With: Joseph Schildkraut, Barbara Kent, Edward G. Robinson.

Star reporter follows adventurous path to solve payroll robbery and double murder.

Roadhouse Nights

Paramount. Directed by Hobart Henley. Scenario and dialogue by Garrett Fort. Story by Ben Hecht.* With: Helen Morgan, Charles Ruggles, Fred Kohler.

After boozing reporter fails, colleague exposes bootlegger's control of town.

Sisters

Columbia. Directed by James Flood. Story by Ralph Graves. Scenario and dialogue by Jo Swerling.* With: Sally O'Neill, Molly O'Day, Russell Gleason.

Protagonists retire to respectability through small country newspaper.

Young Man of Manhattan

Paramount. Directed by Monta Bell. Adaptation by Robert Presnell,* from a book by Katharine Brush. Dialogue by Daniel Reed. With: Claudette Colbert, Norman Foster, Ginger Rogers.

Sportswriter marries movie columnist, then is tempted by socialite, but regains self-esteem through colleague.

1931

Dance, Fools, Dance

MGM. Directed by Harry Beaumont. Scenario by Auriana Rouveral, from the play by Martin Flavin. With: Joan Crawford, Lester Vail, Cliff Edwards.

Socialite becomes sob sister after the crash, saves brother, and gets respect catching gangsters (w/ echoes of Jack Lingle case & St. Valentine's case).

The Finger Points

Warner Brothers/First National. Directed by John Francis Dillon. Story by John Mark Saunders* and W. R. Burnett. With: Richard Barthelmess, Fay Wray, Regis Toomey.

Reporter paid $35 to write and $1000 not to write is finally killed over story by unhappy gangsters (Jake Lingle case).

Five Star Final

Warner Brothers. Directed by Mervyn LeRoy. Adaptation by Robert Lord, from a story by Louis Weitzenkorn.* Dialogue by Byron Morgan. With: Edward G. Robinson, Frances Starr, H.B. Warner.

Editor pushed for scandal copy by publisher and circulation manager causes suicides and destroys innocent lives.

The Front Page

United Artists. Directed by Lewis Milestone. Screenplay by Bartlett Cormack, with dialogue by Bartlett Cormack and Charles Lederer. Based on the play by Ben Hecht* and Charles MacArthur.* With: Adolphe Menjou, Pat O'Brien, Mary Brian.

The archetype. Reporter and editor battle each other, mayor, sheriff, as they seek scoop on condemned man who escapes jail.

Platinum Blonde

Columbia. Directed by Frank Capra. Story by Harry E. Chandler and Douglas W. Churchill.* Dialogue by Robert Riskin.* With: Jean Harlow, Robert Williams, Loretta Young.

Newsrooms more appealing than ballrooms to reporter who marries a socialite.

The Rasp

(GB) Film Engineering (Fox). Directed by Michael Powell. Screenplay by J. Jefferson Farjeon. With: Claude Horton and Phylis Loring.

Reporter proves minister was killed by business rival.

Scandal Sheet

Paramount. Directed by John Cromwell. Story by Vincent Lawrence.* With: George Bancroft, Clive Brook, Kay Francis.

Tyrannical and relentless editor kills wife's banker beau, then dictates story to scoop opposition and land himself in jail.

The Secret Six

MGM. Directed by George Hill. Story by Francis Marion.* With: Wallace Beery, Johnny Mack Brown, Clark Gable.

Reporter gathers information for secret vigilante committee which breaks bootlegging racket.

Sob Sister

Fox. Directed by Alfred Santell. From the book by Mildred Gilman. With: Linda Watkins, James Dunn, Minna Bombell.

Sob sister proves herself to colleagues at expense of her own happiness.

The Star Reporter

Film Engineering (Fox). Directed by Michael Powell. Screenplay by S. Philip Macdonald and Ralph Smart. With: Harold French and Isla Bevan.

Reporter poses as chauffeur to regain girl's stolen jewels.

1932

Blessed Event

Warner Brothers. Directed by Roy Del Ruth.* Screenplay by Howard Green.* From the play by Manuel Senf* and Forrest Wilson. With: Lee Tracy, Dick Powell, Mary Brien.

Unscrupulous columnist is still strong enough to stand up to thugs.

The Crusader

Majestic. Directed by Frank Strayer. From a play by Wilson Collison. With: Ned Sparks, H.B. Warner, Evelyn Brent.

Reporter seeks to expose shady background of crusading DA's wife.

Double Dealing

(GB) Real Art (Fox). Directed by Leslie Hiscott. Screenplay by Michael Barringer and H. Fowler Mear. With: Frank Pettingel and Richard Cooper.

Reporter finds watch committee censor spends wild weekends in London.

The Famous Ferguson Case

Warner Brothers. Directed by Lloyd Bacon. Screenplay by Courtney Terrett* and Harvey Thew,* from a story by Granville Moore. With: Joan Blondell, Tom Brown, Adrienne Dore.

Murder is a side issue as scandal sheet reporters are pilloried and their methods contrasted with those of decent dailies.

The Final Edition

Columbia. Directed by Howard Higgin. From a story by Roy Chanslor.* With: Mae Clark, Pat O'Brien, Mary Doran.

Sob sister fights with unreasonable editor over murder story.

Hollywood Speaks

Columbia. Directed by Edward Buzzell. Screenplay by Edward Buzzell and Norman Krasna.* With: Pat O'Brien, Genevieve Tobin, Lucien Prival.

Hollywood reporter helps girl get screen test.

Is My Face Red?

RKO. Directed by William Seiler. Screenplay by Allen Rivkin.* From the play by Allen Rivkin* and Ben Markson.* With: Ricardo Cortez, Helen Twelvetrees, Robert Armstrong.

Vain, unscrupulous columnist breaks murder story and gets in trouble with both police and crooks.

Love is a Racket

First National. Directed by William Wellman. Adaptation by Courtney Terrett.* From a novel by Rian James.* With: Douglas Fairbanks, Jr., Lee Tracy, Frances Dee.

Stories, dames, and drinks with Broadway columnist whose cynicism covers heart of gold.

Merrily We Go To Hell

Paramount. Directed by Dorothy Arzner. From a book by Cleo Lucas. With: Frederic March, Sylvia Sydney, Adrienne Allen.

Reporter who writes a play wins girl even though he can't stop drinking.

Okay, America

Universal. Directed by Tay Garnett. Story and screenplay by William Anthony McGuire. With: Lew Ayres, Maureen O'Sullivan, Louis Calhern.

Reporter nicknamed Ego writes column in conflict with both publisher and police.

Scandal for Sale

Universal. Directed by Russell Mack. From a novel by Emile Henry Gavreau (Hot News). With: Pat O'Brien, Charles Bickford, Rose Hobart.

Editor neglects family to build circulation, even sending reporter on risky ocean flight to take him out of the way.

Sleepless Nights

(GB) BIP (Wardour). Directed by Thomas Bentley. Screenplay by Victor Kedndall. With: Stanley Lupino and Polly Walker.

Reporter poses as heiress's husband and saves her from eloping with thief.

The Strange Love of Molly Louvain

First National. Directed by Michael Curtiz. Adaptation by Erwin Gelsey and Brown Holmes, from the play by Maurine Watkins. With: Lee Tracy, Ann Dvorak, Richard Cromwell.

Nice reporter helps a lady with a past.

War Correspondent

Columbia. From a story by Keene Thompson. With: Ralph Graves, Jack Holt.

Reporter unmasks fake Chinese war lord.

White Face

(GB) Gainsborough-British Lion (W & F). Directed by T. Hayes Hunter. Screenplay by Angus MacPhail, Brian Edgar Wallace. With: Hugh Williams and Gordon Harker.

Reporter solves murder of crook who blackmailed ex-wife's husband.

1933

Advice to the Lovelorn

20th/Fox. Directed by Alfred Werker. Loosely based on Miss Lonely Hearts *by Nathaniel West. With: Lee Tracy, Sterling Holloway.*

Drunken reporter demoted to lovelorn columnist, where he solves crimes.

Boss Tweed

Columbia. Featuring Charles Coburn. First of thirteen projected "March of the Years" films.

Dramatized version of true 1871 incident when George Jones, first publisher of the New York Times, was offered bribe by Boss Tweed; bribe refused, the *Times* published its story and broke the power of the Tweed ring.

Clear All Wires

MGM. Directed by George Hill. From a play by Bella and Samuel Spewack. ★ *With:*

Braggart head of Chicago paper's foreign news service seeks fame and stories in French colony, Russia, China.

Doss House

(GB) Sound City (MGM). Directed by John Baxter. Screenplay by Herbert Ayres. With: Frank Cellier and Arnold Bell.

Reporter and detective pose as tramps to catch escaped convict.

Falling for You

(GB) Gainsborough (W & F). Directed by Jack Hulbert and Robert Stevenson. Screenplay by Jack Hulbert and Sidney Gilliat. With: Jack Hulbert and Cicely Courtneidge.

Rival reporters don disguises to catch runaway heiress.

Headline Shooters

RKO. Directed by Otto Brower. Screenplay by Allen Rivkin. ★ *Story by Wallace West. With: William Gargan, Frances Dee, Ralph Bellamy.*

Newsreel reporters are rivals for the same story. Atmosphere and narrative reminiscent of *The Front Page.*

I Cover the Waterfront

United Artists. Directed by James Cruze. From a book by Max Miller. With: Ben Lyon, Claudette Colbert, Ernest Torrence.

Reporter exposes smuggling racket run by girlfriend's father.

Mr. Broadway

[A Times Square Travelogue]. Directed by Johnnie Walker. Featuring Ed Sullivan.

Follows Sullivan through three nightclubs as he gathers information for his column. Celebrities include Jack Dempsey, Ruth Etting, Bert Lahr, Hal Le Roy, Joe Frisco, Josephine Dunn, Gus Edwards, Jack Haley, Lupe Velez, Maxie Rosenbloom.

No Marriage Ties

RKO. Directed by J. Walter Ruben. From a

*play by Arch Gaffney and Charles W. Curran.
With: Richard Dix, Elizabeth Allan, Alan
Dinehart.*
The reporter as lush: becomes an advertising
man.

The Picture Snatcher
*Warner Brothers. Directed by Lloyd Bacon.
Screenplay by Allen Rivkin.* Story by Danny
Ahern. With: James Cagney, Ralph Bellamy,
Patricia Ellis.*
Ex-con working for tabloid takes sneak
pictures, including execution photo; all is
well when he gets photo of murderer in
action (based on New York Daily News
scandal).

State Fair
*Fox. Directed by Henry King. From a book by
Philip Duffield Strong. With: Lew Ayres,
Janet Gaynor, Will Rogers.*
On a visit to a fair, a family's daughter is
swept off her feet by a dashing reporter.

Strictly in Confidence
*(GB) Warner Brothers-First National (WB).
Directed by Clyde Ashbrook. With: James
Finlayson and Reginald Purdell.*
Reporters catch confidence trickster.

The World Gone Mad
*Majestic. Directed by William 'Christy'
Cabanne. Screen story by Edward T. Lowe,
Jr. With: Pat O'Brien, Evelyn Brent, Neil
Hamilton.*
Ace reporter catches crooked banker.

1934

The Feathered Serpent
*(GB) GS Enterprises (Col). Directed by Mac-
Lean Rogers. Screenplay by MacLean Rogers
and Kathleen Butler. With: Enid Stamp-
Taylor and Tom Helmore.*
Reporter proves actress did not murder
fence.

Friends of Mr. Sweeney
*Warner Brothers. Directed by Edward Lud-
wig. Screenplay by Warren Duff and Sidney
Sutherland from the novel by Elmer Davis.
Added dialogue by F. Hugh Herbert and
Erwina Gelsey. With: Charlie Ruggles, Ann
Dvorak, Eugene Pallette.*
Meek reporter emboldened by booze ex-
poses small town's crooked politician much
to the dismay of his publisher.

The Hell Cat
*Columbia. Produced by Sid Rogell, from a
story by Adele Buffington. With: Robert Armstrong, Ann Sothern.*
Reporter saves socialite turned sob sister
from crooks.

Hi, Nellie!
*Warner Brothers. Directed by Mervyn LeRoy.
Screenplay by Roy Chanslor* and Abem Fink-
el. Produced by Robert Presnell.* With: Paul
Muni, Glenda Farrell, Berton Churchill.*
Editor who fouls up story demoted to
lovelorn columnist; turns it into hit column
and vindicates himself through scoop.

Hold That Girl
Fox. With: Claire Trevor, James Dunn.
Sob sister rescued from jewel thieves by
detective.

I'll Tell the World
Universal. Produced by Dale van Every.
Original story by Lincoln Quarberg* and
Frank Wead. With: Lee Tracy, Roger Pryor.*
Globe-trotting reporter finds dirigible, res-
cues queen, and reports on a revolution.

It Happened One Night
*Columbia. Directed by Frank Capra. Screen-
play by Robert Riskin* from a story by Samuel
Hopkins Adams. With: Clark Gable, Claudet-
te Colbert, Walter Connolly.*
Runaway heiress meets journalist on a bus.

The Scoop
*(GB) B & D - Paramount British. Directed by
Maclean Rogers. Screenplay by Gerald
Geraghty and Basil Mason. With: Anne Grey
and Tom Helmore.*
Reporter reveals he killed jealous traveller in
self-defence.

Thirty Day Princess
*Paramount. Directed by Marion Gering. From
a story by Clarence Buddington Kelland.*
With: Cary Grant, Sylvia Sidney.*
Editor falls for actress impersonating prin-
cess.

1935

After Office Hours
*MGM. Directed by Robert Z. Leonard.
Screenplay by Herman J. Mankiewicz* from
an original story by Lawrence Stallings* and
Dale van Avery.* With: Clark Gable, Const-
ance Bennett.*
Romance of socialite reporter and editor as
she solves scandal in prominent family.

Behind the Evidence
Columbia. Story and screenplay by Harold Shumate. With: Norman Foster.*
Society reporter solves crimes.

The Bride Comes Home
Paramount. Directed by Wesley Ruggles. Screenplay by Claude Binyon, from a story by Elisabeth Saxany Holding. With: Fred Mac-Murray, Claudette Colbert, Robert Young.*
Penniless socialite in triangle with two men starting magazine.

The Crouching Beast
(GB) Stafford (Radio). Directed by Victor Hanbury. Screenplay by Valentine Williams. With: Fritz Kortner and Wynne Gibson.
American girl reporter helps British spy steal plans of Dardanelles fortifications.

The Daring Young Man
Fox. Directed by Willam S. Seiter. Story by Claude Binyon and Sidney Skolsky.* Screenplay by William Hurlbut. Aditional dialogue by Sam Hellman* and Glenn Tryon. Produced by Robert T. Kane.* With: James Dunn, Mae Clarke, Neil Hamilton.*
Rival reporters assigned to uncover prison conditions find crooks hiding out in jail.

Front Page Woman
Warner Brothers. Directed by Michael Curtiz. Screenplay by Roy Chanslor, Lillie Hawyard and Laird Doyle, from a story by Richard MacAulay. With: Bette Davis, George Brent, Winifred Shaw.*
Competing male and female reporters doublecross each other before true love wins out.

The Gilded Lily
Paramount. Directed by Wesley Ruggles. Screenplay by Claude Binyon, from a story by Melville Baker and Jack Kirkland. With: Fred MacMurray, Claudette Colbert, Ray Milland.*
Girl who rejects British peer made celebrity by reporter, whom she later marries.

The Headline Woman
Mascot. Presented by Nat Levine. Story and screenplay by Jack Natteford and Claire Church. With: Roger Pryor.*

It's a Bet
(GB) BIP (Wardour). Directed by Alexander Esway. Screenplay by L. DuGarde Peach, Frank Miller, and Kurt Siodmak. With: Gene Gerrard and Helen Chandler.
Reporter wins bet by hiding from editor for a month.

Life Begins at Forty
Fox. Directed by George Marshall. Screenplay by Lamar Trotti. Dialogue by Robert Quillan, from a book by Walter Boughton Pitkin. With: Will Rogers, Jane Darwell, Rochelle Hudson.*
One-man newspaper's editor dispenses homilies, advice, and still captures crooks.

Late Extra
(GB) Fox British. Directed by Albert Parker. Screenplay by Fenn Sherie and Ingram D'Abbes. With: James Mason and Virginia Cherrill.
Cub reporter catches fugitive gunman.

Murder Man
MGM. Directed by Tim Whelan. Screenplay by Tim Whelan and John S. Higgins. Story by Tim Wheland and Guy Bolton. With: Spencer Tracy, Virginia Bruce, Lionell Atwill.
Embittered reporter commits murder and puts blame on enemy who killed his parents; at execution interview, reporter confesses own guilt.

$1,000 a Minute Republic.
Directed by Audrey Scotto. Story by Everett Freeman. Screenplay by Joseph Fields. Adaptation by Jack Nattefore* and Claire Church. With: Roger Pryor, Leila Hyams, Edgar Kennedy.*
Comedy of reporter trying to spent $1,000 a minute for twelve hours to settle bet between millionaires.

The Pay-Off
First National. Directed by Robert Florey. Story by Samuel Shipman. Screenplay by George Brisker and Joel Sayre. With: James Dunn, Claire Dodd, Patricia Ellis.*
Sports columnist is in debt to gamblers.

The Riverside Murder
(GB) Fox British. Directed by Albert Parker. Screenplay by Leslie Landau and Selwin Johnson. With: Basil Sidney and Judy Gunn.
Woman reporter helps inspector solve deaths of three financiers on eve of group shareout.

1936

Adventure in Manhattan
Columbia. Directed by Edward Ludwig. From a play by Anita B. Fairgrieve and Helena Miller. With: Joel McCrea, Jean Arthur.
Reporter solves crimes and falls in love with actress.

Big Brown Eyes
Paramount. Directed by Raoul Walsh. Screenplay by Raoul Walsh and Bert Hanlon, from a story by James Edward Grant. With: Joan Bennett, Cary Grant, Walter Pidgeon.
Manicurist who instantly becomes reporter-columnist-editorial writer solves crimes with lovelorn detective's help.

Exclusive Story
MGM. Directed by George B. Seitz. Screenplay by Michael Fessier,* from a story by Martin Mooney.* With: Franchot Tone, Madge Evans, Stuart Erwin.
Reporter helps special prosecutor break rackets. Based on Mooney's experience in New York: suggests Morro Castle fire caused by policy racketeers. Very topical at the time.

Florida Special
Paramount. Directed by Ralph Murphy. Screenplay by David Boe, Marguerite Roberts,* and Laura and S.J. Perelman. Story by Clarence Buddington Kelland.* With: Jack Oakie, Sally Eilers, Kent Taylor.
Reporter chases jewel thieves on train.

Gentle Julia
20th/Fox. Directed by John Blystone. Screenplay by Lamar Trotti,* from a story by Booth Tarkington. With: Jane Withers, Tom Brown, Marsha Hunt.
In Tarkingtonesque small town, child foils saccharine suitor and links aunt up with doubting cub reporter.

The Girl on the Front Page
Universal. Directed by Harry Beaumont. Screenplay by Austin Parker,* Albert R. Perkins, and Alice D.G. Miller. Story by Marjorie and Roy Chanslor.* With: Edmund Lowe, Gloria Stewart, Reginald Owen.
Managing editor runs afoul of girl who inherits newspaper.

The Golden Arrow
First National. Directed by Alfred E. Green. Adaptation by Charles Kenyan, from a play by Michael Arlen. With: Bette Davis, George Brent, Eugene Palette.
Fake heiress set for publicity campaign marries reporter sent for story.

Half Angel
20th/Fox. Directed by Sydney Landfield. Screenplay by Gene Fowler* and Bess Meredyth. Story by F. Tennyson Jesse. With: Brian Donlevy, Frances Dee, Charles Butterworth.

Reporter singlehandedly clears girl of murder charge.

Human Cargo
20th/Fox. Directed by Allan Dwan.* Screenplay by Jefferson Parker and Doris Malloy, from a book by Kathleen Shepard. With: Brian Donlevy, Claire Trevor, Alan Dinehart.
Rival reporters seek to break smuggling ring.

Jailbreak
Warner Brothers. Directed by Nick Grinde. Adaptation by Robert D. Andrews and Joseph Hoffman.* Story by Jonathan Finn. With: Craig Reynolds, June Travis, Barton MacLane.
Reporter solves crimes while in jail.

Libelled Lady
MGM. Directed by Jack Conway. Screenplay by Maurine Watkins, Howard Emmet Rogers, and George Oppenheimer. Story by Wallace Sulliivan. With: Jean Harlow, Spencer Tracy, William Powell.
"Married" reporter woos heiress to stop her libel suit; editor winds up with "wife" and reporter with heiress.

Love on the Run
MGM. Directed by W.S. Van Dyke. Screenplay by John Lee Mahin, Manuel Senff,* and Gladys Hurlbut. Story by Alan Green and Julian Brodie. Produced by Joseph Mankiewicz.* With: Clark Gable, Franchot Tone, Joan Crawford.
Rival European correspondents chase both dame and spy ring.

Man Hunt
Warner Brothers. Directed by William Clemens. Screenplay by Roy Chanslor.* Story by Earl Felton. With: William Gargan, Ricardo Cortez.
Country editor chases gangsters in competition with fleet of ace city reporters and GIs.

Missing Girls
Chesterfield. Directed by Phil Rosen. Screenplay by Martin Mooney* and John W. Krafft.* Story by Martin Mooney.* With: Roger Pryor, Muriel Evans, Sydney Blackmer.
Reporter, in jail for contempt of court, unearths plot to kill Senator and scores scoop.

Mr. Deeds Goes to Town
Columbia. Directed by Frank Capra. Screenplay by Robert Riskin,* from a book by

Clarence Buddington Kelland. * With: Gary Cooper, Jean Arthur, George Bancroft.*
Sudden hick millionaire gets involved with big-city sob sister.

Murder With Pictures
Paramount. Directed by Charles Barton. Screenplay by John C. Moffitt and Sidney Salkow. From a book by George Harmon Coxe. With: Lew Ayres, Gail Patrick, Joyce Compton.*
When cops hold press boys as suspects in series of murders, photographer hides plates revealing guilty party.

Next Time We Love
Universal. Directed by Edward H. Griffith. * Screenplay by Melville Baker, from a book by Ursula Parrott. With: Margaret Sullivan, James Stewart, Ray Milland.*
Stage loses an actress as foreign correspondent persuades his wife to globe-trot with him after stories.

Nothing Like Publicity
(GB) GS Enterprises (Radio). Directed by MacLean Rogers. Screenplay by Kathleen Butler and H.F. Maltby. With: Billy Hartnell and Marjorie Taylor.
Press agent has dud actress pose as American heiress who is also impersonated by a crook.

Road Gang
Warner Brothers. Directed by Louis King. Screenplay by Dalton Trumbo. Story by Abem Finkel and Harold Buckley. With: Donald Woods, Kay Linaker.
Reporter who starts exposé falsely sent to chain gang by crooked politicians; prisoners riot and take him to DA.

Sinner Take All
MGM. Directed by Errol Taggart. Screenplay by Leonard Lee and Walter Wise. From a book by Elwyn Whitman Chambers. With: Dorothy Kilgallen, Bruce Cabot, Margaret Lindsay.
Newspaper crime scandal, made after Kilgallen achieves fame by reporting around-the-world trip for father's paper.

Someone at the Door
(GB) BIP (Wardour). Directed by Herbert Brenon. Screenplay by Jack Davies and Marjorie Deans. With: Billy Milton and Aileen Marson.
Reporter inherits house and fakes murder that comes true.

Two Against the World
Warner Brothers. Directed by William McGann. Screenplay by Michael Jacoby, from the play Five Star Final *by Louis Weitzenkorn.* * With: Humphrey Bogart, Beverly Roberts, Helen MacKellar.*
Remake of *Five Star Final* set in radio journalism, where rehash of old murder case causes suicides, and radio commission cleans up station programming.

Wedding Present
Paramount. Directed by Richard Wallace. Story by Paul Gallico. Produced by B.P. Schulberg. * With: Lew Ayres, Cary Grant, Joan Bennett.*
City editor determined not to lose sob sister to dull suitor.

We're Only Human
RKO. Directed by James Flood. Screenplay by Rian James, * from a story by Thomas Walsh. Produced by Edgar Kaufman.* * With: Jane Wyatt, Preston Foster, James Gleason.*
Woman reporter meets tough but honest cop.

Wife Versus Secretary
MGM. Directed by Clarence Brown. Screenplay by Norman Krasna, * from a book by Faith Baldwin. Additional screenplay by Alice Duer Miller and John Lee Mahin. Produced by Hunt Stromberg.* * With: Clark Gable, Jean Harlow, Myrna Loy.*
Publisher caught in triangle between wife and secretary.

A Woman Rebels
RKO. Directed by Mark Sandrich. Screenplay by Anthony Veiller and Ernest Vajda. From a book by Nitta Syrett. With: Katharine Hepburn, Herbert Marshall, Elizabeth Allan.*
A woman fights for independence in the face of Victorian conventions.

Woman Trap
Paramount. Directed by Harold Young. Screenplay by Brian Marlow and Eugene Walter. * Story by Charles Brackett. With: George Murphy, Gertrude Michael, Sidney Blackmer.*
Reporter chases jewel thieves through Mexico.

Women Are Trouble
MGM. Directed by Earl Taggart. Screenplay by Michael Fessier. * Story by George Harmon Coxe. Produced by Lucien Hubbard and Michael Fessier.* *

With: Stuart Erwin, Paul Ketty, Florence Rice.

1937

Back in Circulation
Warner Brothers. Directed by Ray Enright.* Adaptation by Warren Duff. Story by Adela Rogers St. John. With: Pat O'Brien, Joan Blondell, Margaret Lindsay.
Editor makes life rough but romantic for woman reporter.

Behind the Headlines
RKO. Directed by Richard Rosson. Screenplay by J.R. Bren and E.L. Hartman. Story by Thomas Ahearn.
Renegade G-man devoted to the gold standard captured by demon newsgetter and competing sob sister girlfriend.

Death Croons the Blues
(GB) St. Margaret's (MGM). Directed by David MacDonald. Screenplay by H. Fowler Mear. With: Hugh Wakefield and Antoinette Cellier.
Drunken reporter proves Lady's missing brother did not kill girl singer.

Exclusive
Paramount. Directed by Alexander Hall. Story by John C. Moffitt.* Screenplay by Rian James,* John C. Moffitt* and Sidney Salkow. Produced by Benjamin Glazer.* With: Fred MacMurray, Frances Farmer, Charlie Ruggles.
Newspapers feud after racketeer buys rival paper, causing turmoil in town.

Fly-Away Baby
Warner Brothers. Directed by Frank McDonald. Screenplay by Don Ryan and Kenneth Gant. (Second in Torchy Blane series.) Story by Dorothy Kilgallen.* With: Glenda Farrell, Barton MacLane, Gordon Oliver.
Woman reporter solves murder.

Gangway
Gaumont (GFD). Directed by Sonnie Hale. Screenplay by Lesser Samuels and Sonnie Hale. With: Jessie Matthews and Barry MacKay.
Woman reporter poses as star's maid and is mistaken for Jewel thief.

Headline Crasher
Ambassador. Directed by Peter B. Kyne. Story by Peter B. Kyne. Produced by Maurice Cohn. With: Frankie Darro.

The House of Silence
(GB) George King (MGM). Directed by R.K. Nelson Baxter. Screenplay by Paul White. With: Tom Helmore and Terence de Marney.
Reporter unmasks innkeeper as chief smuggler.

I Cover the War
Universal. Directed by Arthur Lubin. Screenplay by George Waggner. Original story by Bernard McCornville. With: John Wayne, Gwen Gaze, Don Barclay.
Newsreel cameraman in Mesopotamia crushes Arab revolt.

The Last Gangster
MGM. Directed by Edward Ludwig. Screenplay by John Lee Mahin. Story by William A. Wellman and Robert Carson. With: James Stewart, Rose Stradner, Edward G. Robinson.
Gangster serves time and returns home to reclaim wife and child from protection of respectable newspaperman.

Love Is News
20th/Fox. Directed by Tay Garnett. Screenplay by Harry Tugend and Jack Yellen.* Story by William R. Lipson and Frederick Stephani. Produced by Earl Carroll* and Harold Wilson. With: Loretta Young, Tyrone Power, Don Ameche.
Heiress marries snooping reporter to teach him a lesson about being in the public eye.

The Mutiny of the Elsinore
(GB) Argyle British (ABPC). Directed by Roy Lockwood. Screenplay by Waler Summers and Beaufoy Milton. With: Paul Lukas and Lyn Harding.
Reporter aboard ship gets involved in mutiny.

Night Club Scandal
Paramount. Directed by Ralph Murphy. Screenplay by Lillie Hayward. From a play by Daniel N. Rubin. With: Lynne Overman, Louise Campbell, John Barrymore.
Ace reporter disproves circumstantial case against innocent man and captures real killer.

Nothing Sacred
Selznick International. Directed by William Wellman. Screenplay by Ben Hecht.* With: Frederic March, Carole Lombard, Walter Connolly.
Opportunist reporter and editor make celebrity of dying girl to boost circulation; when she is well, they are stuck.

Sensation
(GB) BIP (ABFC). Directed by Brian Desmond Hurst. Screenplay by Dudley Leslie, Marjorie Deans, and William Freshman. With: John Lodge and Diana Churchill.
Reporter solves murder of waitress at village inn.

Smart Blonde
Warner Brothers. Directed by Frank McDonald. Screenplay by Don Ryan and Kenneth Gannet. Story by Frederick Nebel. With: Glenda Farrell, Barton MacLane, Winfred Shaw.
Woman reporter solves mystery of who murdered nightclub owner. First of the Torchy Blane series.

There Goes My Girl
RKO. Directed by Ben Holmes. Screenplay by Harry Segall. Original Story by George Beck. With: Gene Raymond, Ann Sothern, Joseph Crehan.
Editor determined to prevent star woman reporter's marriage to antic reporter for rival paper. (Compared in reviews to *The Front Page*.)

Wake Up and Live
20th/Fox. Directed by Sidney Langfield. Screenplay by Harry Tugend and Jack Yellen.* Story by Curtis Kenyon, from a book by Dorothea Brande. With: Ben Bernie, Walter Winchell, Alice Faye.
Exploits newspaper "feud" between Winchell and Bernie as they chitchat through musical.

Wild Money
Paramount. From a story by Paul Gallico. With: Edward Everett Horton.
Comedy as small-town newspaper hits big, big story.

Women Men Marry
MGM. Directed by Errol Taggart. Screenplay by Donald Henderson Clarke, James Grant and Harry Ruskin. Story by Matt Taylor. Produced by Michael Fessier.* With: George Murphy, Sidney Blackmer, Claire Dodd.
Editor has affair with reporter's wife.

1938

Blondes At Work
Warner Brothers. Directed by Frank McDonald. Screenplay by Albert de Mord. With: Glenda Farrell, Barton MacLane, Tom Kennedy.

(Third in Torchy Blane series.) Woman reporter sent to jail for contempt of court, but still solves murder of department store owner.

Double or Quits
(GB) Warner Brothers - First National (WB). Directed by Roy William Neill. Screenplay by Michael Barringer. With: Frank Fox and Patricia Medina.
Reporter is double of thief who steals rare stamps on transatlantic liner.

Exposed
Universal. Directed by Harold Schuster. Screenplay by Charles Kaufman and Franklin Cohen. Original story by George R. Bilson. With: Glenda Farrell, Otto Kruger, Herbert Mindin.
Woman photographer uncovers disgraced lawyer and helps him capture racketeers who ruined him.

Four's A Crowd
Warner Brothers. Directed by Michael Curtiz. Original story by Allace Sullivan. Adaptation by Casey Robinson and Sig Jerzig. With: Errol Flynn, Rosalind Russell, Olivia de Haviland.
Editor chases sob sister and heiress, ends up with printer's ink.

A Girl With Ideas
Universal. Directed by S. Sylvan Simon. Screenplay by Bruce Manning* and Robert T. Shannon. Original story by William Rankin. With: Kent Taylor, Wendy Barrie, Walter Pidgeon.
Managing editor crosses wits with woman who inherits newspaper.

I See Ice
(GB) ATP (ABFD). Directed by Anthony Kimmins. Screenplay by Anthony Kimmins and Austin Melford. With: George Formby and Kay Walsh.
Gormless employee at ice rink tries to break into Fleet Street as a photographer.

King of the Newsboys
Republic. Directed by Bernard Vorhaus. Screenplay by Louis Weitzenkorn* and Peggy Thompson. Original story by Samuel Ornitz and Horace McCoy. With: Lew Ayres, Helen Mack, Alison Skipworth.

The Last Barricade
(GB) Fox British. Written and directed by Alex Bryce. With: Frank Fox and Greta Gynt.
Reporter saves spy's daughter from prison.

Love and Hisses
20th/Fox. Directed by Sidney Lanfield. Screenplay by Art Arthur* and Curtis Kenyon. With: Ben Bernie, Simone Simone, Walter Winchell.
Exploits newspaper "feud" between Bernie and Winchell, now over new girl singer.

Making the Headlines
Columbia. Directed by Lewis D. Collins. Screenplay by Howard J. Green* and Jefferson Parker. Story by Howard J. Green.* With: Jack Holt, Beverly Roberts, Craig Reynolds.

Mr. Satan
(GB) Warner Brothers - First National (WB). Directed by Arthur Woods. Screenplay by John Meehan, Jr. and J.O.C. Orton. With: Skeets Gallagher and James Stephenson.
War correspondent loves daughter of 'dead' armaments king.

Newsboy's Home
Universal. Directed by Harold Young. Screenplay by Gordon Kahn.* Original story by Gordon Kahn* and Charles Grayson. With: Jackie Cooper, Wendy Barrie, Edmund Loew.
Editor beats female owner of paper to story amid streetfights among flocks of rival newsboys.

Personal Secretary
Universal. Directed by Otis Garrett. Original story by B. Laidlaw and Robert Lively. Produced by Max Gordon. With: William Gargan and Andy Devine.
Reporters help clear small-town girl from gossip about her relationship to murdered ladies' man.

Scandal Street
Paramount. Directed by James Hogan. Story by Vera Caspary.* Produced by Edward T. Lowe. With: Lew Ayres, Roscoe Karns, Louise Campbell.
Reporters help clear small-town girl from gossip about her relationship to murdered ladies' man.

The Sisters
Warner Brothers. Directed by Anatol Litvak. Story by Myron Brinig. Adaptation by Milton Krims.* With: Bette Davis, Errol Flynn, Anita Louise.
Rough married life of reporter who travels and drinks.

Special Edition
(GB) Redd Davis (Par). Directed by Redd
Davis. Screenplay by Katharine Stroeby. With: Lucille Lisle and John Garrick.
Reporter proves photographer stabbed doctor and blackmailer.

There Goes My Heart
Hal Roach (UA). Directed by Norman Z. McLeod. Screenplay by Jack Jevne and Eddie Moran. Original story by Ed Sullivan.* With: Frederic March, Virginia Bruce, Patsy Kelly.
Runaway heiress and snoopy reporter done once again (copycat of It Happened One Night).

This Man Is News
(GB) Pinebrook (Par). Directed by David MacDonald. Screenplay by Allan MacKinnon, Roger MacDougal, and Basil Dearden. With: Barry K. Barnes and Valerie Hobson.
Wife helps framed reporter unmask gem thieves.

Time Out for Murder
20th/Fox. Directed by H. Bruce Humberstone. Screenplay by Jerry Cady. Story by Irving Reis. Produced by Howard J. Green.* With: Michael Whalen, Gloria Stuart, Chick Chandler.
Reporter solves murder and saves innocent man.

Torchy Blane in Panama
Warner Brothers. Directed by William Clemens. Scenario by Anthony Coldeway. With: Lola Lane, Paul Kelly, Tom Kennedy.
(Fourth in Torchy Blane series.) Woman reporter solves murder of bank teller that requires trip to Panama.

Torchy Gets Her Man
Warner Brothers. Directed by William Beaudine. Scenario by Albert De Mord. With: Glenda Farrell, Barton MacLane, Tom Kennedy.
(Fifth in Torchy Blane series.) Woman reporter Farrell brings counterfeiter to justice.

While New York Sleeps
20th/Fox. Directed by H. Bruce Humberstone. Screenplay by Francis Hyland and Albert Ray. Original story by Frank Fenton and Lynn Root. With: Michael Whalen, Chick Chandler, Jean Rogers.
Reporters beat police and rivals to criminal.

1939

Blackwell's Island
Warner Brothers. Directed by William McGown. Scenario by Crane Wilbur. Story by

Crane Wilbur and Lee Katz. With: John Garfield, Rosemary Lane, Dick Purcell.

Reporter sentences himself to prison, then escapes to tell world what happens inside. Exposé based on 1934 raid on Welfare Island prison.

Cafe Society

Paramount. Directed by Edward H. Griffith.* Story and screenplay by Virginia van Upp. With: Fred MacMurray, Madeleine Carroll, Allyn Joslyn.

Socialite marries ship news reporter on a bet.

Confidential Lady

(GB) Warner Brothers - First National (WB). Directed by Arthur Woods. Screenplay by Brock Williams and Derek Twist. With: Ben Lyon and Jane Baxter.

Jilted reporter helps jilted girl thwart press-lord who ruined her father.

Each Dawn I Die

Warner Brothers. Directed by William Keighley. Screenplay by Norman Reilly Raine, Warren Duff, and Charles Perry. From a book by Jerome Odlum.* With: James Cagney, George Raft, Jany Bryan.

Crusading reporter framed and sent to prison, where he helps engineer jailbreak to clear his name.

Everything Happens at Night

20th/Fox. Directed by Irving Cummings. Screenplay by Art Arthur* and Robert Harani. With: Robert Cummings, Ray Milland, Sonja Henie.

Rival newshounds seek anti-Nazi intellectual by wooing his daughter.

Mr. Smith Goes to Washington

Columbia. Directed by Frank Capra. Story by Lewis R. Foster. Screenplay by Sidney Buchman. With: James Stewart, Jean Arthur, Thomas Mitchell.

Idealistic young politician is helped by reporter to learn wiles of Washington. Personal appearance by H.V. Kaltenborn.

Nancy Drew, Reporter

Warner Brothers. Directed by William Clemens. Screenplay by Kenneth Gannet, from stories by Carolyn Keene. With: Bonita Granville, Frankie Thomas, John Litel.

Journalism's turn in the series.

News Is Made at Night

20th/Fox. Directed by Alfred Werker. Screenplay by John Larkin.* Story by John Larkin.

Produced by Edward Kaufman.* With: Lynn Bari, Preston Foster, Russell Gleason.

Novice gal reporter and brusque editor save innocent man from gallows.

Off the Record

Warner Brothers. Directed by James Flood. Screenplay by Lawrence Kimble,* Earl Baldwin, Niven Busch. Original story by Saul Elkins and Sally Sandlin. With: Pat O'Brien, Joan Blondell, Bobby Jordan.

After slot-machine exposé sends kid to reform school, woman reporter marries editor and adopts kid.

Scandal Sheet

Columbia. Directed by Nick Grinde. Original story by Joseph Carole. Produced by Ralph Conn. With: Otto Kruger, Ona Munson.

Sued for Libel

RKO. Directed by Leslie Goodwins. Screenplay by Jerry Kady. Original story by Wolfe Kaufman. With: Kent Taylor, Linda Hayes, Lillian Bond.

Reporter captures killers to cancel unjust libel suit.

Stanley and Livingstone

20th/Fox. Directed by Henry King. Screenplay by Sam Hellman,* Philip Dunne, Julien Josephson.* Story by Sam Hellman* and Hal Long. Produced by Kenneth MacGowan.* With: Spencer Tracy, Nancy Kelly, Richard Greene.

"Story of one of the great journalistic achievements of the last century."

Tell No Tales

MGM. Directed by Leslie Fenton. Screenplay by Lionel Hauser. Story by Pauline London and Alfred Taylor. With: Melvyn Douglas, Louise Platt, Esther Dale.

Editor of dying newspaper makes own headlines by catching kidnapper.

They Asked For It

Universal. Directed by Frank McDonald. Screenplay by Arthur T. Harman. Story by James B. Lowell. With: William Lundigan, Michael Whalen, Jay Hodges.

College kids take over newspaper and stir up excitement with murder hoax.

This Man in Paris

(GB) Pinebrook (Par). Directed by David MacDonald. Screenplay by Allan MacKinnon and Roger MacDougall. With: Barry K. Barnes and Valerie Hobson.

Wife helps reporter unmask bank-note forger.

Torchy Blane in Chinatown

Warner Brothers. Directed by William Beaudine. Scenario by George Brisker. Story by Will Jenkins. With: Glenda Farrell, Barton Mac-Lane, Henry O'Neil.

(Sixth in Torchy Blane series.) No Chinatown, but woman reporter solves series of murders connected with importing jade curios.

Torchy Plays with Dynamite

Warner Brothers. Directed by Noel Smith. Screenplay by Earle Snell and Charles Belden. Story by Scott Littleton. With: Jane Wyman, Allen Jankins, Tom Kennedy.

(Eighth and last in Torchy Blane series, with Wyman replacing Farrell.) Woman reporter deliberately goes to prison to get information from girlfriend of escaped bandit.

Torchy Runs for Mayor

Warner Brothers. Directed by Ray McCarey. Screenplay by Earle Snell, from an idea by Irving Rubine. With: Glenda Farrell, Barton MacLane, Frank Shannon.

(Seventh in Torchy Blane series.) Woman reporter exposes underworld baron who controls city.

1940

Behind the News

Republic. Directed by Joseph Santley. Screenplay by Isabel Dawn and Boyce De Gaw. Produced by Robert North. With: Lloyd Nolan, Doris Davenport, Robert Armstrong.

Young reporters indict crooked DA in face of elder colleague's cynicism.

Comrade X

MGM. Directed by King Vidor. Screenplay by Ben Hecht* and Charles Lederer. Story by Walter Reisch. With: Clark Gable, Hedy Lamarr, Oscar Homolka.

American correspondent in Moscow involved with glamourous streetcar conductress, still gets stories.

Double Alibi

Universal. Directed by Philip Rosen. Screenplay by Harold Buchman and Charles Grayson. Story by Frederick C. David. With: Wayne Morris, Margaret Lindsay, Roscoe Karns.

Accused reporter must show evidence is not pointed at him alone.

Foreign Correspondent

United Artists. Directed by Alfred Hitchcock. Original story by Charles Bennett and Joan Harrison. dialogue by James Hilton and Robert Benchley. With: Joel McCrea, Lorraine Day, Herbert Marshall.

European adventures and suspense with fifth column plot.

His Girl Friday

Columbia. Directed by Howard Hawks. Screenplay by Charles Lederer, from the play The Front Page *by Ben Hecht* and Charles MacArthur.* With: Cary Grant, Rosalind Russell, Ralph Bellamy.*

The Archetype redone.

No Time for Comedy

Warner Brothers. Directed by William Keighley. Screenplay by Julius and Philip Epstein.* From a Play by Samuel N. Behrman.* With: James Stewart, Rosalind Russell.

Small-time reporter's adventures in New York as playwright.

The Philadelphia Story

MGM. Directed by George Cukor. Screenplay by Donald Ogden Stewart, from a play by Philip Barry. Produced by Joseph Mankiewicz. With: Cary Grant, Katharine Hepburn, James Stewart.

Household of rich offbeats invaded by journalists.

1941

Citizen Kane

RKO. Directed by Orson Welles. Original screenplay by Herman J. Mankiewicz and Orson Welles. With: Orson Welles, Joseph Cotton, Dorothy Comingore.

Builder of publishing empire hopes to rule the world.

Confirm or Deny

20th/Fox. Directed by Archie Mayo. Story by Henry Wales* and Sam Fuller.* Screenplay by Jo Swerling.* With: Don Ameche, Joan Bennett.

(Mayo replaced uncredited Fritz Lang.) U.S. reporter in London has invasion plans but can't publish.

Design for Scandal

MGM. Directed by Norman Taurog. Screenplay by Lionel Hauser.* Produced by John W. Considine, Jr. With: Walter Pidgeon, Edward Arnold, Rosalind Russell.

Reporter tries to smear woman judge with gossip, ends up in matrimony.

A Dispatch From Reuters

Warner Brothers. Directed by William Dieterle. Screenplay by Milton Krims.* Story by

Valentine Williams and Wolfgang Wilhelm. With: Edward G. Robinson, Eddie Albert, Edna Best.
Biography of Paul Julius Baron Reuter and his news agency.

East of Picadilly
(GB) ABPC (Pathe). Directed by Harold Huth. Screenplay by Lesley Storm and J. Lee Thompson. With: Judy Campbell and Sebastian Shaw.
Novelist and girl reporter unmask silk-stocking strangler.

Meet John Doe
Warner Brothers. Directed by Frank Capra. Screenplay by Robert Riskin.* Story by Richard Connell and Robert Presnell.* With: Barbara Stanwyck, Gary Cooper, Edward Arnold.
Sob sister invents suicide character, only to be trapped by her own publisher, who wants to manipulate story.

Nine Lives Are Not Enough
Warner Brothers. Directed by A. Edward Sutherland. Screenplay by Fred Niblo, Jr.,* from book by Jerome Odlum.* With: Ronald Reagan, Ed Brophy, Joseph Creham.
Brash, unscrupulous reporter fired for inaccuracies, stays on murder case, and winds up editor when socialite girlfriend buys paper.

Penny Serenade
Columbia. Directed by George Stevens. Screenplay by Morrie Ryskind. Story by Martha Cheevers. With: Cary Grant, Irene Dunne, Beulah Bondi.
Adoption tearjerker: itinerant reporter buys small-town paper and lives in fiscal and emotional crisis.

The Saint's Vacation
(GB) RKO-Radio. Directed by Leslie Fenton. Screenplay by Jeffrey Dell and Leslie Charteris. With: Hugh Sinclair and Sally Gray.
Woman reporter helps detective save sound detector from spies.

Unholy Partners
MGM. Directed by Mervyn LeRoy. Screenplay by Earl Baldwin, Bartlett Cormack, Lesser Samuels. Produced by Samuel Marx. With: Edward G. Robinson, William T. Orr, Edward Arnold.
1920s. Reporter starts own tabloid with backing from crook, who blackmails protégé and is killed by editor, who flies Atlantic with mad pilot and is lost at sea when protege takes over paper.

Washington Melodrama
MGM. Directed by S. Sylvan Simon. Screenplay by Marion Parsonnei and Roy Chanslor,* from a play by L. Durocher Macpherson. With: Kent Taylor, Ann Rutherford, Frank Morgan.
Congressman, reporter, and romance in Washington.

Wide Open Town
Paramount. Directed by Leslie Selander. From characters by Clarence E. Mulford. With: William Boyd, Morris Ankrum.
Hopalong Cassady helps harassed newspaper editor rid community of outlaws.

1942

Berlin Correspondent
20th/Fox. Directed by Eugene J. Forde. Original story by Steve Fisher and Jack Andrews. With: Dana Andrews, Virginia Gilmore, Mona Maris.
Hindsight helps story of international intrigue.

The Day Will Dawn
(GB) Niksos Films (GFC). Directed by Harold French. Screenplay by Terence Rattigan, Anatole de Grunwald and Patrick Kirwan. With: Hugh Williams and Deborah Kerr.
US title: **The Avengers.**
Reporter and skipper's daughter destroy U-boat base and are rescued by commandos.

I Was Framed
Warner Brothers. Directed by D. Ross Lederman. Screenplay by Robert E. Kent. Story by Jerome Odlum.* With: Michael Ames, Julie Bishop, Regis Toomey.
Crusading reporter breaks jail to nab crooked politicians.

Journey for Margaret
MGM. Directed by W.S. Van Dyke. Screenplay by David Hertz and William Ludwig, from a book by William Lindsay White. With: Lorraine Day, Robert Young, Margaret O'Brien.
War correspondent and wife flee France, adopt war orphan in England.

Keeper of the Flame
MGM. Directed by George Cukor. Screenplay by Donald Ogden Stewart, from a novel by Ida Alexa Ross Wylie. With: Spencer Tracy, Katharine Hepburn, Richard Whorf.

Star reporter searches for true nature of dead hero; first suppresses story of hero's fascism, then prints all.

The Lady Has Plans
Paramount. Directed by Sidney Lanfield. Screenplay by Harry Tugend. Story by Leo Nirinski. With: Ray Milland, Paulette Goddard, Roland Young.
Female correspondent in Lisbon is taken for a spy.

The Man Who Came To Dinner
Warner Brothers. Directed by William Keighley. Screenplay by Julius J. and Philip G. Epstein, from the play by George S. Kaufman and Moss Hart. With: Monty Wooley, Ann Sheridan, Richard Travis.
Convalescent tyrant meddles in romance between his secretary and reporter.

Once Upon a Honeymoon
RKO. Directed by Leo McCarey. Original story by Sheridan Gibney* and Leo McCarey. With: Cary Grant, Ginger Rogers, Walter Slezak.
American reporter in Warsaw rescues American chorus girl married to Nazi villain.

Roxie Hart
20th/Fox. Directed by William A. Wellman. Screenplay by Nunally Johnson,* from a play by Maurine Watkins. With: Ginger Rogers, George Montgomery, Adolphe Menjou.
Fake murder arrest for publicity becomes serious when politics of electorate becomes involved.

Somewhere I'll Find You
MGM. Directed by Wesley Ruggles. Adapted by Walter Reisch from a story by Charles Hoffman. With: Robert Sterling, Clark Gable, Lana Turner.
Asian-correspondent brothers love same woman until one is killed reporting at Bataan.

Shadow of the Thin Man
MGM. Directed by W.S. Van Dyke. Screenplay by Harvey Kuruitz* and Irving Brecher. From characters by Dashiell Hammett.* With: Myrna Loy, William Powell, Barry Nelson.
Sporting world of gamblers, touts, and bookies.

Suspected Person
(GB) ABPC (Pathe). Written and directed by Lawrence Huntingdon. With: Clifford Evans and Patricia Roc.
Swindled reporter finds American bank robber's loot and is stopped from keeping it by his sister.

They All Kissed the Bride
Columbia. Directed by Alexander Hall. Original story by Gina Claus and Andrew P. Salt. Produced by Edward Kaufman. With: Joan Crawford, Roland Young, Billie Burke.
Formidable businesswoman terrorizes employees and family until social-minded reporter humanizes her.

Thunder Rock
(GB) Charter (MGM) Directed by Roy Boulting. Screenplay by Wolfgang Wilhelm, Jeffrey Dell, Bernard Miles and Anna Reiner, from a play by Robert Ardrey.
A writer rejects the world and peoples his lighthouse with the victims of an 1849 shipwreck.

Unpublished Story
(GB) Two Cities (Col). Directed by Harold French. Screenplay by Anatole de Grunwald and Patrick Kirwan. With: Richard Greene and Valerie Hobson.
Reporter exposes pacifist organization as Nazi saboteurs.

Uncensored
(GB) Gainsborough (GFD). Directed by Anthony Asquith. Screenplay by Wolfgang Wilhelm, Terence Rattigan and Rodney Ackland. With: Eric Portman and Phyllis Calvert.
Editor writes for both Nazi paper and secret news-sheet run by patriots.

Woman of the Year
MGM. Directed by George Stevens. Screenplay by Ring Lardner, Jr.,* and Michael Kanin. Produced by Joseph Mankiewicz.* With: Spencer Tracy, Katharine Hepburn, Fay Bainter.
Sports columnist and world affairs woman reporter marry, find careers in conflict.

You Can't Escape Forever
Warner Brothers. Directed by Jo Graham. Story by Roy Chanslor.* Screenplay by Fred Niblo, Jr.* and Hector Chevigny. With: George Brent, Brenda Marshall, Paul Garvey.
Remake of Hi, Nellie.

1943

Headline
(GB) John Cornfield (Ealing). Directed by John Harlow. Screenplay by Ralph Gilbert Bettinson and Maisie Sharman. With: Anne

Crawford and David Farrar.
Reporter finds editor's wife is missing witness to woman's murder.

Johnny Come Lately
United Artists. Directed by William K. Howard. From a book by Louis Bromfield. Screenplay by John van Druten. With: James Cagney, Gladys George, Marjorie Mann.
Itinerant reporter helps old lady keep small-town crooks from doing in her one-woman paper.

Power of the Press
Columbia. Directed by Lew Landers. Screenplay by Robert D. Andrews. Story by Samuel Fuller.★ With: Lee Tracy, Otto Kruger, Guy Kibbee.

They Got Me Covered
United Artists. Directed by David Butter. Screenplay by Harry Kurnitz.★ Story by Leonard Q. Ross★ (Pseud. Leo C. Rosten) and Leonard Spiegelgass. With: Bob Hope, Dorothy Lamour, Otto Preminger.
Disgraced correspondent called back to Washington, gets involved with spies.

What a Woman
Columbia. Directed by Irving Cummings. Original story by Eric Charell. Produced by Sidney Buchman. With: Rosalind Russell, Brian Aherne.
Magazine writer profiles author's agent and ends in matrimony.

1944

Arsenic and Old Lace
Warner Brothers. Directed by Frank Capra. Screenplay by Julius J. and Philip G. Epstein, from a play by Joseph Kesselring. With: Cary Grant, Raymond Massey, Jack Carson.
Theatre critic finds whole family is killed.

It Happened Tomorrow
United Artists. Directed by René Clair.★ Screenplay by Dudley Nichols.★ Original story by Hugh Wedlock, Howard Snyder, Lord Dunsany. With: Dick Powell, Linda Darnell, Jack Oakie. 1900.
Young reporter gets scoops by tracing facts from tomorrow's newspaper, delivered by ghost.

Lady in the Dark
Paramount. Directed by Mitchell Leisen. Screenplay by Frances Goodrich and Albert Hackett, from a play by Moss Hart, Kurt Weil,

and Ira Gershwin. With: Ginger Rogers, Ray Milland, Jon Hall.
Fashion editor dreams of new, more feminine lives with interesting men.

Laura
20th/Fox. Directed by Otto Preminger. Screenplay by Jay Drather, Samuel Hoffenstein, and Betty Reinhardt. From a book by Vera Caspary.★ With: Clifton Webb, Vincent Price, Judith Anderson.
Critic becomes interpreter of dead girl's life.

1945

Blood on the Sun
United Artists. Directed by Frank Lloyd. Screenplay by Lester Cole. Original story by Garrett Fort. Idea by Frank Melford. With: James Cagney, Sylvia Sidney, Wallace Ford.
Prewar correspondent in Tokyo forsees aggression; when ignored, he takes on militarists himself.

Christmas in Connecticut
Warner Brothers. Directed by Peter Godfrey. Screenplay by Lionel Houser★ and Adele Commandim. Story by Aileen Hamilton. With: Barbara Stanwick, Dennis Morgan, Sydney Greenstreet.
Homemaking columnist assigned to entertain returning war hero, falls in love.

Crime, Inc.
Producer's Releasing Company. Directed by Lew Landers. Screenplay by Roy Schrock, from a book by Martin Mooney★ (also assoc. prod.). With: Tom Neal, Lionel Atwell, Leo Carillo.
Reporter faces jail for refusing to divulge information, but still gets crooks.

Dumb Dora Discovers Tobacco
(GB) Hurley (GN). Directed by Charles Hawtrey. Screenplay by Victor Katona and Henry King. With: Henry Kendall and Pamela Stirling.
Girl reporter researches into history of smoking.

Eve Knew Her Apples
Columbia. Directed by Will Jason. Screenplay by E. Edwin Moran. Story by Rian James.★ With: Ann Miller, William Wright, Robert Williams.
Remake of *It Happened One Night.*

Here Comes the Sun
(GB) John Baxter (GFD). Directed by John

Baxter. Screenplay by Geoffrey Orme. With:
Bud Flanagan and Chesney Allen.
Tipster breaks jail to prove he was framed
by crooked newspaper proprietor.

Men of the Mines
(GB) Bruton (Premier). Directed by David
Mackane. Screenplay by Edward Cork. With:
Ernest Butcher and Gladys Young.
Reporter falls for miner's daughter.

Midnight Manhunt
Paramount. Directed by William Thomas.
Screenplay by David Lang. Produced by
William Pine⋆ and William Thomas. With:
William Gargan, Ann Savage, Leo Gorcey.

State Fair
20th/Fox. Directed by Walter Lang. Screen-
play by Oscar Hammerstein II. Adaptation by
Sonya Levien⋆ and Paul Green⋆ Story by Phil
Strong. With: Dana Andrews, Jeanne Crain,
Dick Haynes.
Musical remake of 1933 version.

The Story of G.I. Joe
United Artists. Directed by William Wellman.
Screenplay by Leopold Atlas, Guy Endore,
Philip Stevenson.
Based on the wartime journalism of Ernie
Pyle.

1946

Deadline for Murder
20th/Fox. Directed by James Tinling. Story
and screenplay by Irvin Cummings, Jr. With:
Kent Taylor, Paul Kelley, Sheila Ryan.
Woman reporter solves crimes.

Easy to Wed
MGM. Directed by Edward Buzzell. Screen-
play by Dorothy Kingsley. With: Keenan
Wynn, Lucille Ball, Van Johnson.
Remake of *Libelled Lady.*

The Glass Alibi
Republic. Produced and directed by W. Lee
Wilder. Screenplay by Minred Lord. With:
Apul Kelly, Douglas Fowley, Anne Gwynne.
Reporter tries to commit perfect crime, but
is caught.

Her Kind of Man
Warner Brothers. Directed by Frederick de
Cordova. Screenplay by Gordon Kahn⋆ and
Leopold Atlas. Original story by Charles Hoff-
man and James V. Kern. Produced by Alex
Gottlieb.⋆ With: Dane Clark, Janis Page,
Zachary Scott.
Sleuthing Broadway columnist solves crime.

Late at Night
(GB) Bruton Films (Premier). Directed by
Michael Chorlton. Screenplay by Henry C.
James. With: Daphne Day and Barry Morse.
Singer helps reporter catch the leader of a
wood-alcohol gang.

Perilous Holiday
Columbia. Directed by Edward H. Griffith.⋆
Screenplay by Roy Chanslor,⋆ from a magazi-
ne serial by Robert Carson. With: Pat
O'Brien, Ruth Warrick, Alan Hale.
Reporter and playboy team up to catch
crooks.

The Searching Wind
Paramount. Directed by William Dieterle.
Screenplay and play by Lillian Hellman.
With: Robert Young, Sylvia Sydney, Ann
Richards.
Sob sister warns of fascism, is dismissed by
idealist diplomat who later regrets it.

The Walls Came Tumbling Down
Columbia. Directed by Lothar Mendes. Screen-
play by Wilfred H. Pettitt. From a book by Jo
Eisinger. With: Lee Bowman, Marguerite
Chapman, Edgar Buchanan.
Columnist investigates the death of a priest.

1947

Brighton Rock
(GB) Associated British/The Boultings.
Directed by John Boulting. Screenplay by
Graham Greene and Terence Rattigan.
with: Richard Attenborough and Hermione
Baddeley.
Brighton gangster murders investigative re-
porter and attempts coverup.

The Corpse Came C.O.D.
Columbia. From a book by Jimmy Starr.⋆
With: George Brent, Joan Blondell, Jim
Bannon.

Crime Reporter
(GB) Knightsbridge-Hammer (Exclusive).
Directed by Ron R. Hart. Screenplay by
James Corbett. With: John Blythe and George
Denhurst.
Reporter unmasks Soho black marketeer
behind taxicab murder.

Gentlemen's Agreement
20th/Fox. Directed by Elia Kazan. Screenplay
by Moss Hart, from a book by Laura Z.
Hobson. With: Gregory Peck, Celeste Holm,
Nicholas Joy.

Reporter poses as Jew to find out about discrimination.

The Guilt of Janet Ames
Columbia. Directed by Charles Vidor. Original story by Lenore Coffee. With: Melvyn Douglas.
The reporter as lush.

The Hangman Waits
(GB) Five Star (Butcher). Written and directed by A. Bark-Smith. With: John Turnbull and Anthony Baird.
Inspector and reporter track down organist who killed usherette.

Magic Town
RKO. Directed by William Wellman. Screenplay by Robert Riskin. Story by Robert Riskin* and Joseph Krumgold. With: James Stewart, Jane Wyman, and Kent Smith.*
Media exploits the "perfect" small town.

News Hounds
Monogram. Produced by Jan Grippo. Story by Edmond Sewards, Tim Ryan, and George Cappy.*

The Private Affairs of Bel Ami
UA. Written and directed by Albert Lewin. With: George Sanders and Angela Lansbury.
A career journalist climbs to fame over the ruined lives of his friends.

So Well Remembered
(GB) Alliance (RKO) Directed by Edward Dmtyryk. Screenplay by by John Paxton, from the novel by James Hilton. With: John Mills, Martha Scott, Patricia Roc.
Idealistic editor marries and divorces an ambitious mill-owner.

1948

All Over the Town
(GB) Rank/Wessex. Written and directed by Derek Twist. With: Norman Wooland and Sarah Churchill.
Two reporters revive local newspaper and expose local corruption.

The Big Clock
Paramount. Written and directed by John Farrow. From a book by Kenneth Fearing. With: Charles Laughton, George MacReady, Henry Morgan.
Murder in the world of magazine publishing.

Call Northside 777
20th/Fox. Directed by Henry Hathaway.

Based on an article by James P. McQuire. With: James Stewart, Richard Conte, Lee J. Cobb.*
True story. Reporter becomes convinced of innocence of man jailed for eleven years.

It Hapened in Soho
(GB) FC Films (ABFC) Directed by Frank Chiswell. Screenplay by Terry Sanford. With: Richard Murdoch and Patricia Raine.
Reporter unmasks Soho strangler.

June Bride
Warner Brothers. Directed by Bretagne Windust. Screenplay by Ronald MacDougall. From a play by Eileen Tight and Graeme Lorimer. With: Bette Davis, Robert Montgomery, Fay Bainter.
Lady editor and dusty foreign correspondent disrupt marriage in small town while on assignment.

The Luck of the Irish
20th/Fox. Directed by Henry Koster. From a book by Guy Pearce Jones and Constance Bridges Jones. With: Tyrone Power, Jayne Meadows, Ann Baxter.
Reporter torn between boss's daughter and Irish colleen.

On Our Merry Way
United Artists. Directed by King Vidor and Leslie Fenton. Story by Arch Oboler and John O'Hara. With: Burgess Meredith, Paulette Goddard, Fred MacMurray.
Episodes in the life of classified clerk who wants to become reporter.

1949

Abandoned
Universal. Directed by Joseph M. Newman. Story and screenplay by Irwin Gielgud. With: Dennis O'Keefe, Gale Storm, Jeff Chandler.
Reporter breaks baby-adoption racket.

Chicago Deadline
Paramount. Directed by Lewis Allen. Screenplay by Warren Duff. From a book by Tiffany Thayer. With: Alan Ladd, June Havoc, Donna Reed.
Reporter solves crimes.

The House Across the Street
Warner Brothers. Directed by Richard L. Bare. Screenplay by Russell Hughes. Story by Roy Chanslor. With: Wayne Morris, Janis Paige, Bruce Bennett.*
Reporter solves murder in remake of Hi, Nellie.

Malaya
MGM. *Directed by Richard Thorpe. Screenplay by Frank Fenton. Story by Manchester Boddy. With: Spencer Tracy, James Stewart.*
Government taps correspondent to help smuggle rubber out of Malaya and past Japanese.

Marry Me
(GB) Gainsborough (GFD). Directed by Terence Fisher. Screenplay by Lewis Gilbert and Denis Waldock. With: David Tomlinson and Susan Shaw.
Fleet Street reporter is assigned to investigate marriage bureau.

Paper Orchid
(GB) Ganesh (Col). Directed by Roy Baker. Screenplay by Val Guest. With: Hugh Williams and Hy Hazell.
Reporter's confession clear's girl colleague from charge of killing star.

That Wonderful Urge
20th/Fox. Directed by Robert B. Sinclair. Screenplay by Jay Dratler. Story by William R. Lipman and Frederick Stepham. With: Tyrone Power, Gene Tierney, Reginald Gardiner. Remake of Love Is News.

1950

All About Eve
20th/Fox. Written and directed by Joseph Mankiewicz.* From a story and radio play by Mary Orr. With: Bette Davis, Anne Baxter, George Sanders.
Manipulative star-maker shows cold-blooded will in Broadway setting.

Born Yesterday
Columbia. Directed by George Cukor. Screenplay by Albert Mannheimer, from a play by Garson Kanin. With: William Holden, Judy Holliday, Broderick Crawford.
Washington journalist exposes corrupt lobbyist.

Dangerous Assignment
(GB) Target (Apex). Directed by Ben R. Hart. Screenplay by Chuck Messina. With: Lionel Murton and Pamela Deeming.
Girl helps American reporter clean up stolen car racket.

Hangman's Wharf
(GB) Duk Films. Directed by Cecil H. Williamson. Screenplay by John Beldon. With: John Witty and Genine Graham.
Girl reporter helps doctor prove that he did not kill rich man.

Right Cross
MGM. Directed by John Sturges. Story and screenplay by Charles Schnee. With: Ricardo Montalban, Dick Powell, June Allyson.
Melodrama where sportswriter loses girl to boxer.

Room to Let
(GB) Hammer (Exclusive). Directed by Godfrey Grayson. Screenplay by John Gilling and Godfrey Grayson. With: Jimmy Hanley and Valentine Dyall.
Reporter learns that crippled widow's lodger is Jack the Ripper.

Someone at the Door
(GB) Hammer (Exclusive). Directed by Francis Searle. Screenplay by A.R. Rawlinson. With: Michael Medwin and Yvonne Owen.
Reporter and sister inherit old house and invent a murder that comes true.

Summer Interlude (SW; *Sommarlek*)
Written and directed by Ingmar Bergman. With: Maj-Britt Nilsson and Birger Malmsten.
An ageing ballerina with a journalist lover looks back on her youth.

To Please a Lady
MGM. Directed by Clarence Brown. Story and screenplay by Barre Lyndon* and Marge Decker. With: Barbara Stanwyck, Clark Gable.
Sob columnist hounds racing-car diver out of career and then marries him.

The Twenty Questions Murder
(GB) Pax-Pendennis (GN). Directed by Paul Stein. Screenplay by Patrick Kiewan and Victor Katona. With: Robert Beatty and Rona Anderson.
Reporter unmasks killer who sends clues to radio quiz show.

The Underworld Story (AKA The Whipped)
United Artists. Directed by Cyril Endfield. Screenplay by Henry Blankford, from a novel by Craig Rice. With: Dan Duryea, Herbert Marshall, Gale Storm.
When publisher directs suspicion toward innnocent man to shield his own son, reporter prints true story.

1951

Bannerline
MGM. Directed by Don Weis. Screenplay by

Charles Schnee. From a story by Sampson Raphelson. With: Keefe Braselle, Sally Forest, Lionel Barrymore.*
Reporter cleans up town.

The Big Carnival (aka Ace in the Hole)
Paramount. Directed by Billy Wilder. Story and screenplay by Billy Wilder, Lesser Samuels, Walter Newman. With: Kirk Douglas, Jan Sterling, Bob Arthur.
Down-and-out reporter demoted from city to town manipulates mine tragedy scoop to get back to the big time.

Come Fill the Cup
Warner Brothers. Directed by Gordon Douglas. Screenplay by Ivan Gaff* and Ben Roberts. From a book by Harian Ware. With: James Cagney, Phyllis Thaxter, Raymond Massey.
Reporter is reformed alcoholic helping publisher's nephew kick the bottle.

Fort Worth
Warner Brothers. Directed by Edward L. Marin. Story and screenplay by John Twist. Produced by Anthony Veiller.* With: Randolph Scott, Dick Jones, David Brian.
Frontier newsman has to strap on his guns to clean up town.

Here Comes the Groom
Paramount. Directed by Frank Capra. Screenplay by Virginia Van Upp, Liam O'Brien, Myles Connolly, from a story by Robert Riskin* and Liam O'Brien. With: Bing Crosby, Jane Wyman, Franchot Tone.
Roving reporter weds in order to adopt three French orphans.

The Racket
RKO. Directed by John Cromwell. Screenplay by William Wister Haines and W.R. Burnett, from a play by Bartlett Cormack. With: Robert Hutton, Robert Mitchum, Robert Ryan.

1952

Assignment Paris
Paramount. Directed by Robert Parrish. Screenplay by William Bowers.* From a book by Paul Gallico. With: Dana Andrews, Marta Toren, George Sanders.

Captive City
United Artists. Directed by Robert Wise. Screenplay by Alvin M. Josephy, Jr. and Karl Kamb. Story by Alvin M. Josephy, Jr. With: John Forsythe, Joan Camden, Harold J. Kennedy.

Editor trying to break rackets in small city is terrorized and finds friends won't help; runs to Kefauver Committee.

The Case of the Old Rope Man
(GB) Instructional (GFD). Directed by Darrell Catling. Screenplay by Alistair Scobie. With: James Carney and Howell Davies. (short). Reporter solves murder of dockside nightwatchman.

Deadline USA
20th/Fox. Directed and written by Richard Brooks.* Story by Richard Brooks. With: Humphrey Bogart, Ethel Barrymore, Kim Hunter.
Crusading reporter breaks racket by deadline as paper is sold and prints last edition.

Lady in the Fog
(GB) Hammer-Lippert (Exclusive). Directed by Sam Newfield. Screenplay by Orville Hampton. With: Cesar Romero and Lois Maxwell. US title: Scotland Yard Inspector.
American reporter proves woman's brother was not run over accidentally.

Lone Star
MGM. Directed by Vincent Sherman. Screenplay by Howard Estabrook. Story by Borden Chase. With: Clark Gable, Ava Gardner, Broderick Crawford.
Romance of a woman editor in the West.

Park Row
United Artists. Written, directed and produced by Samuel Fuller.* With: Gene Evans, Mary Welch, Bela Kovacs.
The newspaper world and reporting at the turn of the century; Fuller: "The story of my heart."

The San Francisco Story
Warner Brothers. Directed by Robert Parrish. Screenplay by D.D. Beauchamp. From a book by Richard Aldrich Summers. With: Joel McCrea, Yvonne De Carlo, Sidney Blackmer.
Local tycoon joins newspaper and vigilantes to capture crook.

Scandal Sheet
Columbia. Directed by Phil Karlson. Screenplay by Ted Sherdeman, Eugene Ling, and James Peo. From a book by Samuel Fuller.* With: Broderick Crawford, Donna Reed, John Derek.
Editor and staff outwit cops on murder.

The Sell-Out
MGM. Directed by Gerald Mayer. Screenplay by Charles Palmer. Story by Matthew Rapf.

With: Walter Pidgeon, Everett Sloane, Cameron Mitchell.
Kefauver. Editor uses newspaper to root out police corruption in his town.

The Turning Point
Paramount. Directed by William Dieterle. Screenplay by Warren Duff. From a story by Horace McCoy. With: William Holden, Edmond O'Brien, Tom Tully.
Kefauver. Crusading reporter and public investigator team up to break rackets.

Washington Story
MGM. Directed by Robert Pirosh. Screenplay by Robert Pirosh. Produced by Dore Schary.★ With: Van Johnson, Patricia Neal, Louis Calhern.

1953

Francis Covers the Big Town
Universal. Directed by Arthur Lubin. Screenplay by Oscar Brodney. Story by Robert Arthur, based on a character by David Stern. With: Donald O'Connor and Francis the talking mule.
Mule passes along overheard scoops to cub reporter.

Hot News
Allied Artists. Directed by Edward Bernds. Story and screenplay by Charles R. Marion★ and Elwood Ullman.★ With: Stanley Clements, Gloria Henry, Ted De Corsica.

It Happens Every Thursday
Universal. Directed by Joseph Pevney. Screenplay by Dane Lussier. From the autobiography of Jane S. McIlvane.★ With: John Forsythe, Loretta Young, Frank McHugh.
Husband-and-wife team run small-town weekly.

Little Boy Lost
Paramount. Directed by George Seaton. Screenplay by George Seaton, from a book by Margharita Laski. With: Bing Crosby, Claude Dauphin, Christian Fourcade.
Wartime correspondent returns to France to seek illegitimate son he has never seen.

Never Let Me Go
MGM. Directed by Delmer Daves. Screenplay by Ronald Miller and George Fraeschel.★ From a book by Roger Box (pseud: Paul Winterton). With: Clark Gable, Gene Tierney, Bernard Miles.
Moscow correspondent at war's end falls for ballerina, smuggles her past Iron Curtin.

Roman Holiday
Paramount. Directed by William Wyler. Screenplay by Ian Hunter and John Dighton, from a story by Ian McLellan Hunter. With: Gregory Peck, Audrey Hepburn, Eddie Albert.
Reporter woos runaway princess.

1954

The Black Rider
(GB) Balbair (Butcher). Directed by Wolf Rilla. Screenplay by A.R. Rawlinson. With: Jimmy Hanley and Rona Anderson.
Reporter and motor-cycle club catch smugglers 'haunting' ruined castle.

Carnival Story
RKO. Directed by Kurt Neumann. Screenplay by Kurt Neumann and Hans Jacoby. Story by Marcel Klauber and C.B. Williams. With: Anne Baxter, Steve Cochrane, George Nader.
Writer solves murder in carnival.

The Delavine Affair
(GB) Croydon-Passmore (Monarch). Directed by Douglas Pierce. Screenplay by Robert Chapman. With: Peter Reynolds and Honor Blackman.
Reporter framed for killing jewel robbery informant.

Escape by Night
(GB) Tempean (Eros). Written and directed by John Gilling. With: Bonar Colleano and Andrew Ray.
Reporter catches fugitive vice king by pretending to help him.

Final Appointment
(GB) Unit/ACT Films. Directed by Terence Fisher. Screenplay by Sidney Nelson and Maurice Harrison. With: John Bentley and Eleanor Summerfield.
Reporter saves lawyer from being killed by victim of wartime court-martial.

Front Page Story
(GB) Jay Lewis (BL). Directed by Gordon Parry. Screenplay by Jay Lewis, Jack Howells, William Fairchild, and Guy Morgan. With: Jack Hawkins and Elizabeth Allan.
News editor deals with several stories: traitorous scientist, homeless children, euthanasia.

I Cover the Underworld
Republic. Directed by R.G. Springsteen. Screenplay by John K. Butler. With: Ray Middleton, Sean McClory, Joanne Jordan.

Living It Up
*Paramount. Directed by Norman Taurog. Screenplay by Jack Rose and Melville Shavelson, based on a story by Ben Hecht.** Loose remake of *Nothing Sacred*.

Playgirl
Universal. Directed by Joseph Pevney. Screenplay by Robert Blees. Story by Roy Buffum. With: Shelly Winters, Barry Sullivan, Colleen Miller.
Newspapers dig for real story when magazine publisher found dead.

1955

The Big Knife
*United Artists. Directed by Robert Aldrich. Screenplay by James Poe.** From a play by Clifford Odets. With: Jack Palance, Ida Lupino, Shelly Winters.*
Tired Hollywood star hounded by studio head and bitchy columnist.

The Big Tip-Off
Allied Artists. Directed by Frank McDonald. Story and screenplay by Steve Fisher. With: Richard Conte, Constance Smith, Bruce Bennett.
Reporter breaks charity-fund racket and solves murder.

The Gold Express
(GB) Gaumont (RFD). Directed by Guy Ferguson. Screenplay by Jackson Budd. With: Vernon Gray and Ann Walford.
Reporter and wife thwart plan to rob train of gold shipment.

Headline Hunters
Republic. Directed by William Witney. Story and screenplay by Frederick Louis Fox and John Butler. With: Rod Cameron, Julie Bishop, Ben Cooper.

Love Is a Many-Splendored Thing
20th/Fox. Directed by Henry King. Story by Han Suyin. With: William Holden, Jennifer Jones.
Correspondent in Hong Kong falls in love with Eurasian doctor.

One Jump Ahead
(GB) Kenilworth (GFD). Directed by Charles Saunders. Screenplay by Doreen Montgomery.

With: Paul Carpenter and Diane Hart.
Reporter solves deaths of blackmailing girl and schoolboy witness.

The Phenix City Story
Allied Artists. Directed by Phil Karlson. Screenplay by Crane Wilbur and Dan Mainwaring. With: John McIntyre, Richard Kiley, Kathryn Grant.
Dramatization of true-story cleanup of Phenix City, Alabama.

Stolen Assignment
(GB) ACT Films-Unit (BL). Directed by Terence Fisher. Screenplay by Kenneth R. Hayles. With: John Bentley and Hy Hazell.
Reporter and girl prove that woman did not kill her niece.

Texas Lady
*RKO. Directed by Tim Whelan. Story and screenplay by Horace McCoy.** With: Claudette Colbert, Barry Sullivan, Greg Walcott.*
Lady wins at poker, pays father's debts, and takes over inherited Texas newspaper.

Track the Man Down
(GB) Republic Productions. Directed by R.G. Springsteen. Screenplay by Paul Erickson and Kenneth R. Hayles. With: Kent Taylor and Petula Clark.
Reporter catches dogtrack-takings thief on long-distance bus.

1956

Behind the Headlines
(GB) Kenilworth (RFD). Directed by Charles Saunders. Screenplay by Allan MacKinnon. With: Paul Carpenter and Hazel Court.
Reporters solve murder of blackmailing blonde.

The Harder They Fall
Columbia. Directed by Mark Robson. Screenplay by Philip Yordan. Based on a novel by Budd Schulberg. With: Humphrey Bogart, Rod Steiger, Mike Lane.
Sportswriter exposes hoodlums in boxing game.

High Society
MGM. Directed by William Beaudine. From a play by Philip Barry. With: Frank Sinatra, Grace Kelly, Bing Crosby.
Musical remake of *The Philadelphia Story*.

Over-Exposed
Columbia. Produced by Lewis J. Rachmil. Story by Richard Sale and Mary Loos. With:

Richard Crenna, Cleo Moore.
Reporter-photographer on trail of vice ring
turns in photos for a gun.
While the City Sleeps
RKO. Directed by Fritz Lang. Screenplay by
Casey Robinson, from a novel by Charles
Einstein. With: Dana Andrews, Rhonda
Fleming, Salley Forrest.
Top reporters compete for editor's job by
trying to solve series of brutal sex murders.
You Can't Run Away From It
Columbia. Directed by Dick Powell. From a
story by Samuel Hopkins Adams. With: Jack
Lemmon, June Allyson.
Remake of It Happened One Night.

1957

Designing Woman
MGM. Directed by Vincente Minnelli. Story
and screenplay by George Wells. Produced by
Dore Schary.* With: Gregory Peck, Lauren
Bacall, Mickey Shaughnessy.
Crusading sportswriter marries fashion de-
signer, hides out from mobsters.
The Girl in the Picture
(GB) Cresswell (Eros). Directed by Donald
Chaffey. Screenplay by Paul Rogers. With:
Donald Houston and Patricia Holt.
Reporter seeks girl witness to murder of
policeman.
The Great Man
Universal. Directed by José Ferrer. From a
book by Al Morgan. With: José Ferrer and
Keenan Wynn.
Radio journalist finds dead hero was a heel
but can't broadcast story as advertisers want
reputation intact.
Hour of Decision
(GB) Tempean (Eros). Directed by Pennington
Richards. Screenplay by Norman Hudis.
With: Jeff Morrow and Hazel Court.
American reporter proves wife did not
poison blackmailer.
Kill Me Tomorrow
(GB) Delta (Renown). Directed by Terence
Fisher. Screenplay by Robert Falconer and
Manning O'Brine. With: Pat O'Brien and
Lois Maxwell.
Sacked reporter confesses to kiling editor in
return for son's operation.
Murder Reported
(GB) Fortress (Col). Directed by Charles

Saunders. Screenplay by Robert Chapman.
With: Paul Carpenter and Melissa Stribling.
Reporter and boss's daughter solve death of
local councillor.
Slander
MGM. Directed by Roy Roland. Screenplay
by Jerome Weidman, from a teleplay by Harry
W. Junkin. With: Van Johnson, Steve
Cochrane, Ann Blythe.
Scandal publisher blackmails TV star over
imperfect past.
Stranger in Town
(GB) Tempean (Eros). Directed by George
Pollock. Screenplay by Norman Hudis and
Edward Dryhurst. With: Alex Nicol and Anne
Page.
American reporter solves shooting of black-
mailer.
Sweet Smell of Success
United Artists. Directed by Alexander Macken-
drick. Screenplay by Ernest Lehman and
Clifford Odets, from a book by Ernest Lehman.
With: Burt Lancaster, Tony Curtis, Susan
Harrison.
Cynical Broadway columnist and weak press
agent manipulate news.

1958

Another Time, Another Place
(GB) Kaydor (Par). Directed by Lewis Allen.
Screenplay by Stanley Mann. With: Lana
Turner and Barry Sullivan.
Girl reporter assures correspondent's widow
that she did not love him.
The Diplomatic Corpse
(GB) ACT Films (RFD). Directed by Montgomery Tully. Screenplay by Sidney Nelson
and Maurice Harrison. With: Robin Bailey
and Susan Shaw.
Reporter solves diplomat's murder and
rescues kidnapped fiancee from foreign
embassy.
I Want to Live
United Artists. Directed by Robert Wise. Based
on letters of Barbara Graham and newspaper
articles of Ed Montgomery.* With: Susan
Hayward, Simon Oakland.
Reporter builds public hysteria against
woman accused of murder, then tries to
prove her innocence but must watch help-
lessly as she is executed. True story.

Teacher's Pet
Paramount. Directed by George Seaton. Story and screenplay by Fay and Michael Kanin. With: Clark Gable, Doris Day.
Uneducated editor falls for pretty journalism teacher. As a promotion, many U.S. daily newspaper film critics played roles as day extras.

Undercover Girl
(GB) Bill & Michael Luckwell (Butcher). Directed by Francis Searle. Screenplay by Bernard Lewis and Bill Luckwell. With: Paul Carpenter and Kay Callard.
Dead reporter's brother unmasks nightclub owner as blackmailing drug peddler.

A Woman of Mystery
(GB) Danziger (UA). Directed by Ernest Morris. Screenplay by Eldon Howard and Brian Clemens. With: Dermot Walsh and Hazel Court.
Reporter unmasks counterfeit gang behind girl's suicide.

1959

The Angry Hills
(GB) Raymond (MGM). Directed by Robert Aldrich. Screenplay by A.I. Belzerides. With: Robert Mitchum and Elizabeth Muller.
Girl helps wounded American correspondent escape with list of Greek resistance agents.

The Desperate Men
(GB) Merton Park (AA). Directed by Peter Maxwell. Screenplay by James Eastwood. With: Jill Ireland and Conrad Philips.
Gem thief holds girl hostage on old castle to force reporter to help him.

Men of Tomorrow
(GB) Border (NR). Directed by Alfred Travers. Screenplay by Alfred Travers and Vernon Greeves. With: Vernon Greeves, Janet Smith and David Hemmings.
(short) Reporter helps orphan teenagers lose aggressiveness.

--30-- (UK title: Deadline Midnight)
Warner Brothers. Directed by Jack Webb. Screenplay by William Bowers.* With: Jack Webb, William Conrad, David Nelson.
A day in the life of a small-city newspaper as flood story breaks.

1960

Date at Midnight
(GB) Danziger (Par). Directed by Godfrey Grayson. Screenplay by Mark Grantham. With: Paul Carpenter and Jean Aubrey.
American reporter proves lawyer's nephew did not kill girl.

Dead Lucky
(GB) ACT Films (BL). Directed by Montgomery Tully. Screenplay by Sidney Nelson and Maurice Harrison. With: Vincent Ball and Betty McDowall.
Reporter proves girlfirend did not kill amorous gambler.

Identity Unknown
(GB) Danziger (Par). Directed by Frank Marshall. Screenplay by Brian Clemens. With: Richard Wyler and Pauline Yates.
Reporters interview relatives of survivors of plane crash.

Sands of the Desert
(GB) ABPC (NR). Directed by John Paddy Carstairs. Screenplay by John Paddy Carstairs and Charlie Drake. With: Charlie Drake and Sarah Branch.
Travel agent saves girl reporter from sheikh and opens holiday camp in desert.

1961

The Day the Earth Caught Fire
(GB) Melina (Pax). Directed by Val Guest. Screenplay by Wolf Mankowitz and Val Guest. With: Janet Munro and Leo McKern.
Reporter discovers that simultaneous American and Russian nuclear bomb tests have shifted Earth's axis.

The Long Shadow
(GB) Argo (RFD). Directed by Peter Maxwell. Screenplay by Paddy Manning O'Brine. With: John Crawford and Susan Hampshire.
American reporter saves Hungarian rebel's child and Swedish nurse from Nazi working for the Russians.

The Mark
(GB) Stross (20). Directed by Guy Green. Screenplay by Sydney Buchman and Stanley Mann. With: Maria Schell and Stuart Whitman.
Reporter exposes widow's lover as man convicted of sexual assault on young girl.

Out of the Shadow
(GB) Border (NR). Written and directed by Michael Winner. With: Terence London and Donald Gray.
Reporter proves brother's suicide was murder.

Shoot to Kill
(GB) Border (NR). Written and directed by Michael Winner. With: Dermot Walsh and Joy Webster.
Reporters save atomic secrets from communist agents.

1962

Fate Takes a Hand
(GB) Danziger (MGM). Directed by Max Varnel. Screenplay by Brian Clemens. With: Ronald Howard and Christina Gregg.
GPO man and girl reporter deliver letters stolen fifteen years ago.

The Fur Collar
(GB) Albatross (RFD). Written and directed by Lawrence Huntington. with: John Bentley and Martin Benson.
Reporter feigns death to trap fugitive and uncover spy ring.

The Intruder
Pathe-America. Directed by Roger Corman. Screenplay by Charles Beaumont, from his novel. With: William Shatner, Frank Maxwell, Beverly Linsford.
Southern editor tries to calm racial tensions caused by outsider bigots.

Madison Avenue
Twentieth Century-Fox. Directed by Bruce Humberstone. Screenplay by Norman Corwin from a book by Jeremy Kird. With: Dana Andrews, Eleanor Parker, Jeanne Crain.
Success seems assured until manipulated journalist blows the whistle on advertising-agency intrigue.

The Man Who Shot Liberty Valence
Paramount. Directed by John Ford. Screenplay by Willis Goldbeck and James Warner Bellah, from a story by Dorothy M. Johnson. With: James Stewart, John Wayne, Vera Miles.
Reporter finds true story of old case.

State Fair
MGM. Directed by José Ferrer. With: Pat Boone, Ann-Margaret, Bobby Darin.
Second remake of 1933 film.

1963

Critic's Choice
Warner Brothers. Directed by Don Weis. Screenplay by Jack Sher, from a play by Ira Levin. With: Bob Hope, Lucille Ball, Marilyn Maxwell.
Critic debates whether ethics will let him review wife's play. Based loosely on Jean and Walter Kerr.

Echo of Diana
(GB) Butcher's Films. Directed by Ernest Morris. Screenplay by Reginald Hearne. With: Vincent Ball and Betty MacDowall.
Reporters uncover spy ring behind death of woman's husband.

Impact
(GB) Butcher's Films. Directed by Peter Maxwell. Screenplay by Peter Maxwell and Conrad Philips. With: Conrad Philips and George Pastell.
Reporter traps club owner who framed him for robbery.

A New Kind of Love
Paramount. Directed by Melville Shavelson. Story and screenplay by Melville Shavelson. With: Paul Newman, Joanne Woodward.
Jaded columnist on vacation in Paris pursues fashion executive.

Please Don't Eat the Daisies
MGM. Directed by Charles Walters. From a book by Jean Kerr. With: Doris Day, David Niven.
Home life of theatre critic, complicated with family capers.

Shock Corridor
Allied Artists. Directed by Samuel Fuller.* Screenplay by Samuel Fuller.* With: Peter Breck, Constance Towers, Gene Evans.
Reporter poses as patient in mental hospital to solve murder, begins to lose own senses.

1964

Black Like Me
Continental Distributing. Directed by Carl Lerner. Screenplay by Gerda Lerner and Carl Lerner, from a book by John Howard Griffin.* With: James Whitmore, Clifton James, Lenka Peterson.
Story of a white southern editor who lives as a black, based on true account by Griffin.

1965

Be My Guest
(GB) Three Kings-Harold Shampan Filmusic (RFD). Directed by Lance Comfort. Screenplay by Lyn Fairhurst. With: David Hemmings and Avril Angers.
Teenage reporter exposes producer's attempt to rig beat group contest.

Boeing Boeing
Paramount. Directed by John Rich. Screenplay by Edward Anhalt, from a play by Marc Camoletti. With: Jerry Lewis, Tony Curtis.
Comedy of rival foreign correspondents and their girlfriends in Paris.

Dead Man's Chest
(GB) Merton Park (AA). Directed by Patrick Dromgoole. Screenplay by Donald Giltinian. With: John Thaw and Ann Thirbank.
Reporter fakes colleague's murder to expose weakness of circumstantial evidence.

Quick, Before It Melts
MGM. Directed by Delbert Mann. Screenplay by Dale Wasserman, from a novel by Philip Benjamin. With: Robert Morse, George Maharis, Anjanette Comer.
Two New York newsmen study Antarctica and cause international incident.

1966

City of Fear
(GB) Towers of London (Planet). Directed by Peter Bezencenet. Screenplay by Peter Welbeck and Max Bourne. With: Terry Moore and Albert Lieven.
Canadian reporter and American fashion expert smuggle scientist and daughter across border.

The Ghost and Mr. Chicken
Universal. Directed by Alan Rafkin. Screenplay by Jim Fritzell and Everett Greenbaum. With: Don Knotts, Joan Staley, Lion Redmons.
Mystery comedy of shy reporter solving twenty-year-old crime to become hero.

Press for Time
(GB) Titan-Ivy (RFD). Directed by Robert Asher. Screenplay by Norman Wisdom and Eddie Leslie. With: Norman Wisdom and Angela Browne.
PM's grandson becomes reporter on seaside newspaper.

1967

Interlude
(GB) Domono (Col). Directed by Kevin Billington. Screenplay by Lee Langley and Hugh Leonard. With: Oskar Werner and Barbara Ferris.
Woman reporter has affair with married doctor.

1968

Beware the Black Widow
Nadir Films. Directed by Larry Crane. Screenplay by Walter M. Berger. With: Sharon Kent, Don Caulfield, Luke St. Clair.
Editor and reporter solve mafia killings.

Headline Hunters
(GB) Ansus (CFF). Directed by Jonathan Ingrams. Screenplay by Jonathan Ingrams and C.M. Pennington Richards. With: Leonard Brockwell and Susan Payne.
Children run newspaper while father is ill.

The Odd Couple
Paramount. Directed by Gene Saks. Screenplay by Neil Simon, from his play. With: Jack Lemmon, Walter Matthau, John Fiedler.
Neat TV newsman and sloppy divorced sportswriter make an unlikely couple. Later successful TV series.

Strategy of Terror
Universal. Directed by Jack Smight. Screenplay by Robert L. Joseph. With: Barbara Rush, Harry Townes, Hugh O'Brien.
Detective and woman reporter stop plot to destroy UN headquarters.

Z
(FR/ALG) Algeria Reggane/ONCIC/Jacques Perrin. Directed by Costa-Gavras. Screenplay by Costa-Gavras and Jorge Semprun. With: Jean-Louis Trintignant and Jacques Perrin.
A newspaper photographer and a magistrate are determined to uncover the truth behind the mysterious death of an opposition member of parliament.

1969

Gaily, Gaily
United Artists. Directed by Norman Jewison. Screenplay by Abram S. Ginnes, from a book by Ben Hecht.* With: Beau Bridges, Melina Mercouri, Brian Keith.
Based on Hecht's memories as a young

reporter in Chicago, but the snap is out of the brim.

1970

The Firecasers
(GB) ITC (RFD). Directed by Sidney Havers. Screenplay by Philip Levins. with: Chad Everett and Anjanette Comer.
Girl reporter helps insurance detective trap arsonist behind explosive teamakers.

1971

Suburban Wives
(GB) Blackwater Butcher. Written and directed by Derek Ford. With: Eva Whishaw and Maggie Wright. (sex film)
Woman reporter writes seven stories of sex in the suburbs.

1972

The Mattei Affair
(IT: Il Caso Mattei) Directed by Francesco Rosi. Screenplay by Francesco Rosi and Tonino Guerra. With: Gian Maria Volonte and Luigi Squarzina.
The investigation into the death of oil boss Enrico Mattei including a journalist's reconstruction of Mattei's last day.

Young Winston
(GB) Open Road (Columbia-Warner). Directed by Richard Attenborough. Screenplay by Carl Foreman. With: Simon Ward and Robert Shaw.
Lord's son's adventures as a Boer War correspondent.

1973

Big Zapper
(GB) Shonteff (Miracle). Directed by Lindsay Shonteff. Screenplay by Hugh Brody. With: Linda Marlowe and Richard Monette.
(sex film) Woman reporter uses sex to bring murderous pimp to justice.

State of Siege
(FR/IT/FRG: Etat de Siege) Directed by Costa-Gavras. Screenplay by Costa-Gavras and Franco Solinas. With: Yves Montand and Renato Salvatori.
The international press cover the guerilla kidnapping of an American police advisor in Uruguay.

Theatre of Blood
(GB) United Artists/Cineman. Directed by Douglas Hickox. Screenplay by Anthony Greville-Bell. With: Vincent Price, Diana Rigg, Coral Browne, Jack Hawkins.
Barnstorming Shakespearean actor takes his revenge on the London Drama Critics' Circle by murdering its members one by one in ingenious ways.

1974

The Front Page
Universal. Directed by Billy Wilder. Screenplay by Billy Wilder and I.A.L. Diamond. With: Walter Matthaw and Jack Lemmon.
Remake of classic newspaper tale.

The Odessa File
(GB) Domino/Oceanic (Col). Directed by Ronald Neame. Screenplay by Kenneth Ross and George Markstein. With: John Voight and Maximillian Schell.
Journalist uncovers organization assisting ex-SS officers.

The Parallax View
Paramount. Directed by Alan J. Pakula. Screenplay by David Giler and Lorenzo Semple, Jr. With: Warren Beatty and Paula Prentiss.
Journalist fatally uncovers the truth behind political assassination.

1975

All the President's Men
Directed by Alan J. Pakula. Screenplay by William Goldman, based on the book by Carl Bernstein* and Bob Woodward*. With: Robert Redford, Dustin Hoffman, Jason Robards, Jr.
The story of the Watergate break-in and the investivative reporters who got the facts.

The Lost Honor of Katharina Blum
(FRG; Die Verlorene Ehre der Katharina Blum) Directed by Volker Schlöndorff. Screenplay by Volker Schlöndorff and Margarethe Von Trotta. With: Angela Winkler and Mario Adorf.
An apolitical young woman is the innocent victim of a smear campaign by the gutter press.

Posse

Directed by Kirk Douglas. Screenplay by William Roberts and Christopher Knopf. With: Kirk Douglas and Bruce Dern.
A railroad bandit is relentlessly pursued by a marshall, whose motives are questioned by a local newspaperman.

That Lucky Touch

(GB) Gloria (Fox-Rank). Directed by Christopher Miles. Screenplay by John Briley and Monja Danischewsky. With: Roger Moore and Susannah York.
Arms dealer falls for American journalist at NATO war games.

1977

Between the Lines

Midwest Film Productions. Directed by Joan Micklin Silver. With: John Heard, Lindsay Crouse, and Jeff Goldblum.
Staff of underground Boston newspaper worried by commercialization.

1978

Capricorn One

Associated General/Lew Grade. Written and directed by Peter Hyams. With: Elliot Gould and James Brolin.
A reporter discovers that the first manned space flight to Mars was a hoax.

The Green Room

(FR; La Chambre Verte) Written and directed by François Truffaut. With: François Truffaut and Nathalie Baye.
A survivor of the Great War works for a provincial newspaper in France as an obituary writer and is bent on preserving memories of the past.

Rough Treatment

(POL; Bez Znieczulenia) Directed by Andrzej Wajda. Screenplay by Andrzej Wajda. Agnieszka Holland, and Krzystof Zaleski. With: Zbigniew Zadasiewicz and Ewa Dalkowska.
The downfall of an eminent political correspondent, abandoned by the state, his colleagues and family.

Slow Dancing in the Big City

UA. Directed by John Avildsen. Screenplay by Barry Grant. With: Paul Sorvino and Anne Ditchburn.
A New York journalist tries to save an eight

year old heroin addict and falls in love with an afflicted ballerina.

1981

Absence of Malice

Columbia. Directed by Sydney Pollack. Screenplay by Kurt Luedtke.* With: Paul Newman and Sally Field.
Liberal journalist manipulated by FBI to implicate innocents in disappearance of union leader.

Reds

Paramount. Directed by Warren Beatty. Screenplay by Warren Beatty and Trevor Griffiths. With: Warren Beatty and Diane Keaton.
Journalist John Reed and Louise Bryant's experience of the Russian Revolution.

1982

Another Way

(HUN; Egymasra Nezve) Directed by Karoly Makk. Screenplay by Karoly Makk and Erzsebet Galgoczi. With: Jadwiga Jandowska-Cieslak and Grazyna Szapolowska.
A tragic love-affair between a female journalist and a married woman working on a political weekly paper in 1957 Budapest.

1983

Under Fire

Orion. Directed by Roger Spottiswoode. Screenplay by Ron Shelton and Clayton Frohman. With: Gene Hackman, Nick Nolte, and Joanna Cassidy.
Three journalists become dangerously involved in Central American politics.

1984

The Killing Fields

(GB) Enigma/First Casualty/Goldcrest (Col-EMI/Warner). Directed by Roland Joffe. Screenplay by Bruce Robinson. With: Sam Waterston and Haing S. Ngor.
US Journalist is forced to leave his Cambodian assistant behind after the fall of Pnomh Penh.

1985

Defence of the Realm
(GB) London Wave/Enigma (Rank). Directed by David Drury. Screenplay by Martin Stellman. with: Gabriel Byrne and Greta Scacchi.
Reporter exposes scandal involving politician.
Eleni
CBS. Directed by Peter Yates. Screenplay by Steve Tesich. With: Kate Nelligan and John Malkovich.
A New York Times journalist returns to Greece to investigate his mother's death in the civil war.
The Mean Season
Orion. Directed by Philip Borsos. Screenplay by Leon Piedmont. With: Kurt Russell and Mariel Hemingway.
A police reporter in Florida acts as the spokesman for a murderous psychopath.
Perfect
Directed by James Bridges. Screenplay by Aaron Latham and James Bridges. With: John Travolta and Jamie Lee Curtis.
A Rolling Stone journalist questions his own ethics while doing a story on health clubs.

1986

Salvador
Hemdale. Directed by Oliver Stone. Screenplay by Oliver Stone and Richard Boyle. With: James Woods and James Belushi.
Semi-fictionalized account of American journalist's search for a story in El Salvador.

1987

Cry Freedom
(GB) UIP. Directed by Richard Attenborough. Screenplay by John Briley. With: Denzel Washington and Kevin Kline.
Black South African activist killed in prison and white journalist friend flees country with family to bring story to world.
Switching Channels
Directed by Ted Kotcheff. Screenplay by Jonathan Reynolds. With: Kathleen Turner and Burt Reynolds.
The Front Page plot transposed to a cable TV news station.
A World Apart
(GB) Directed by Chris Menges. Screenplay by

Shawn Slove. With: Johdi May and Barbara Hershey.
A liberal journalist balances bringing up her daughters with her political activism.

1988

Eight Men Out
Orion. Written and directed by John Sayles. With: John Cusack, Charlie Sheen, Studs Terkel.
Sports journalists Ring Lardner and Hugh Fullerton cover the 1919 World Series and expose the eight members of the Chicago White Sox team who accepted bribes from gambler Arnold Rothstein to throw the series.

1990

Newshounds
(GB) BBC-TV. Directed by Les Blair. With: Alison Steadman and Adrian Edmundson.
Indictment of ethics in British tabloid journalism.

1991

Hors La Vie (aka Beirut)
Fr/It. Written and directed by Maroud Bagdadi. With: Hippolyte Girardot.
French newspaper cameraman is kidnapped by Islamic fundamentalist group in Beirut and held hostage.

A NOTE ON TELEVISION

In the 1950s some television series used newsmen as leading characters: "Big Town" (1950) had Jane Nigh as crusading editor and aide solving crimes in a series that had been popular with Edward G. Robinson and Claire Trevor on radio; "I Cover Times Square" (1950) had Harold Huber in the role of a Broadway columnist; "Front Page Detective" (1951) featured Edmund Lowe as a crimebusting columnist; "Crime Photographer" (1952) was Darren McGavin; "Wire Service" (1956) saw George Brent and Dane Clark as roving crime solvers; "Big Story" (1956) with Ben Graver dramatized actual stories and saluted the reporters who broke them. The invincible Hi Nellie! theme turned up in "Dear Phoebe" (1954) where Peter Lawford became the comic

lovelorn columnist. Some recent TV resur-
rections of the newspaper genre include
"No. 19 Coronado Drive" (1974), a situation
comedy with Fred MacMurray as a publisher that never got beyond the pilot stage;
Darren McGavin returning in "The Night
Stalker" (1974) as a reporter in the world of
the supernatural; "The Name of the Game"
(1968) had Gene Barry, Robert Stack and
Tony Franciosa rotating in a series which
started with a TV movie called Fame Is the
Name of the Game; "The Andros Targets"
(1977) starred James Sutoris as a worldwide
investigative crimebuster. The most interesting attempt to bring some real newsroom issues before the public on television,
though, was the immensely succcesful "Lou
Grant" series starring Ed Asner as a twofisted yet sympathetic editor of a major
metropolitan daily.

British television has given weekly attention to the press in the longest-running
current affairs programme in TV history –
Granada's "What the Papers Say", which
began in 1956 on ITV, switched in the 1980s
to Channel 4 and is now carried on BBC2.
There has not, however, been much of an
imaginative kind. Contrasted sports jouralists figure in Tom Stoppard's TV play
"Professional Foul" (1977), there has been a
TV version of Michael Frayn's stage play
"Alphabetical Order" (1975), a comedy set
in a provincial newspaper office, and the
hero of David Hare's "Dreams of Leaving"
(1980) about an ambitious reporter coming
to Fleet Street. The first really successful
BBC twice-weekly soap opera "Compact"
(1962-65) was about the lives and loves of
the employees of the eponymous woman's
magazine. Fifteen years later Maureen Lipman starred as the advice page editor of a
women's magazine in the ITV series
"Agony" (1979-81). At that time there was
a BBC series "Shoestring" (1979-80) featuring Trevor Eve as an earnest investigative
reporter for a West Country local radio
station – a decade before such a hero would
have been a newspaperman and as equally
unlikely a character. "Lytton's Diary"
(1985-86), scripted by former Evening Standard journalist Ray Connolly, was devised
by its star Peter Bowles, who modelled his
role on a famous Fleet Street gossip columnist. "Hold the Back Page" (1985), written by Andrew Nickolds and Stan Hey, ran
for ten weeks on the BBC and took in both
ends of the Fleet Street spectrum by having
its hero, an ace sports correspondent played
by David Warner, move from a posh Sunday
paper to a tabloid. "Hot Metal" (1986), was
a tough satire on sleazy tabloid journalism
with Robert Hardy in a dual role.

THE PRESS: OBSERVED AND PROJECTED

This dossier is published to accompany and amplify the material of two Seasons of films organized by the editors at the National Film Theatre, London, in July and October 1991, in honour of the 200th Anniversary of *The Observer*, which began publication on December 4, 1791. Films screened at the NFT in these Seasons included:

––30–– (**Deadline Midnight**) *1959* Directed by Jack Webb
Absence of Malice *1981* Directed by Sydney Pollack
Ace in the Hole *1951* Directed by Billy Wilder
All the President's Men *1975* Directed by Alan J. Pakula
Another Way *1982* Directed by Karoly Makk
Between the Lines *1977* Directed by Joan Micklin Silver
Call Northside 777 *1948* Directed by Henry Hathaway
Circle of Deceit *1981* Directed by Volker Schlöndorff
Citizen Kane *1940* Directed by Orson Welles
Cry Freedom *1985* Directed by Richard Attenborough
The Day the Earth Caught Fire *1961* Directed by Val Guest
Deadline USA *1952* Directed by Richard Brooks
Defence of the Realm *1985* Directed by David Drury
A Dispatch from Reuters *1940* Directed by William Dieterle
Five Star Final *1931* Directed by Mervyn LeRoy
Foreign Correspondent *1940* Directed by Alfred Hitchcock
Fourth Estate *1940* Directed by Paul Rotha
The Front Page *1931* Directed by Lewis Milestone
Front Page Woman *1935* Directed by Michael Curtiz
Front Page Story *1953* Directed by Gordon Parry
The German Sisters *1981* Directed by Margarethe von Trotta
Hi, Nellie! *1934* Directed by Mervyn LeRoy
His Girl Friday *1940* Directed by Howard Hawks
I Cover the Waterfront *1933* Directed by James Cruze

I.F. Stone's Weekly *1972* Directed by Jerry Bruck, Jr.

Judith Therpauve *1983* Directed by Patrice Chereau

The Killing Fields *1984* Directed by Roland Joffe

La Chambre verte (The Green Room) *1978* Directed by François Truffaut

Libelled Lady *1936* Directed by Jack Conway

The Lost Honor of Katharina Blum *1975* Directed by Volker Schlöndorff

Love and Hisses *1937* Directed by Sidney Lanfield

The Man Who Shot Liberty Valence *1962* Directed by John Ford

The Mattei Affair *1972* Directed by Francesco Rosi

Newshounds *1990* Directed by Les Blair

Nine Lives Are Not Enough *1941* Directed by Edward Sutherland

Nothing Sacred *1937* Directed by William A. Wellman

Park Row *1952* Directed by Samuel Fuller

The Philadelphia Story *1940* Directed by George Cukor

Posse *1975* Directed by Kirk Douglas

The Quiet American *1956* Directed by Joseph L. Mankiewicz

Salvador *1983* Directed by Oliver Stone

Scandal Sheet *1931* Directed by John Cromwell

Sensation *1936* Directed by Brian Desmond Hurst

Shock Corridor *1963* Directed by Samuel Fuller

The Story of G.I. Joe *1945* Directed by William A. Wellman

The Sweet Smell of Success *1957* Directed by Alexander Mackendrick

Teacher's Pet *1958* Directed by George Seaton

This Man Is News *1938* Directed by David Macdonald

−−30−− (Deadline Midnight) *1959* Directed by Jack Webb

Un nuage entre les dents *1974* Directed by Marco Pico

Under Fire *1983* Directed by Roger Spottiswoode

Unpublished Story *1942* Directed by Harold French

The Wakefield Express *1952* Directed by Lindsay Anderson

Woman of the Year *1942* Directed by George Stevens

A World Apart *1987* Directed by Chris Menges

SELECT BIBLIOGRAPHY

Barris, Alex. **Stop the Presses! The Newspaperman in American Films**
New York, 1976: A.S. Barnes & Co.
A nostalgic illustrated look at newspaper films.

Bergman, Andrew. **We're in the Money**
New York, 1971: New York University Press
A study of Depression American and its films, contains a section on "a City of Newspapermen".

Courson, Maxwell Taylor. **The Newspaper Movies: An Analysis of the Rise and Decline of the New Gatherer as a Hero in American Motion Pictures, 1900-1974**
(Ph.D. Dissertation, cinema, University of Hawaii, 1976) Ann Arbor, 1977: University Microfilms
A discussion of the role of the reporter in popular films.

Dooley, Roger. **From Scarface to Scarlett**
New York, 1981: Harcourt, Brace, Jovanovich
A study of 1930s American cinema, contains a section "Stop the Press! News Hawks and Sob Sisters".

Ghiglione, Loren. **The American Journalist: Paradox of the Press**
Washington, D.C., 1990: The Library of Congress
Catalogue to accompany the travelling exhibition on the journalist in popular culture.

Ghiglione, Loren. "The reel journalist vs. the real journalist: Hollywood's image of the newspaperman"
The Evening News, *Southbridge, MA, 17 October 1976.*

Gross, Jane. "Movies and the Press Are an Enduring Romance"
The New York Times, *2 June 1985; sec. 2, p. 19.*

Hecht, Ben, & MacArthur, Charles. **The Front Page**
New York, 1928: Covici-Friede Publishers

Kael, Pauline. **The Citizen Kane Book**
Boston, 1971: Little, Brown & Company

Langer-Burns, Heidi M. **The Image of Jouranlists in American Film and Fiction from 1975 to 1987: An Application of Leo Löwenthal's Model**
(Ph.D. Dissertation, School of Journalism, Southern Illinois University, April 1989)

Meisel, Myron. **Dateline . . . Hollywood**
Boston, 1975: Museum of Fine Arts
Notes to the film programme of 1 May – 14 June 1975.

Roffman, Peter, & Purdy, Jim. **The Hollywood Social Problem Film**
Bloomington, 1981: Indiana University Press
A study of American social cinema; contains a section "The Newshawks".

Rossell, Deac. "The Fourth Estate and the Seventh Art" in Bernard Rubin, ed. **Questioning Media Ethics**
New York, 1978: Praeger Publishers

Rossell, Deac. "Hollywood and the Newsroom" in **American Film V. 1 #1, October 1975.**
Essay on the newspaper film genre.

Rotha, Paul. **Documentary Diary**
London, 1973: Secker & Warburg
A collection of reviews and writings on the cinema; this second, expanded edition contains a long essay on the making of Fouth Estate, Rotha's film of *The Times*.

Ryan, Desmond. "The Hollywood Reporter: Movies That Do a Reel Number on the Press", in **Washington Journalism Review, September 1985.**

Van Riper, Frank. "In the Flicks" and Edward C. Norton, "On the Tube" in **"How Hollywood Views the Press", Nieman Reports, vol. XXXIII, No. 4 (Winter 1979).**

Zynda, Thomas H. "The Hollywood Version: Movie Portrayals of the Press" in **Journalism History, vol. 6, No. 1 (Spring 1979).**

A NOTE ON THE CONTRIBUTORS

Michel Cieutat is a critic for *Positif* and teaches American Civilization at the University of Strassbourg. He has written a monograph on Martin Scorsese and is the author of the two-volume Les grande thèmes du cinéma americain.

Philip French has been film critic of *The Observer* since 1978. His books include The Movie Moguls and Westerns: Aspects of a Movie Genre. He is currently working on a monograph about Louis Malle and co-editing (with Ken Wlaschin) The Faber Book of Movie Verse.

Samuel Fuller was a journalist with the New York *Evening Journal*, the New York *Evening Graphic*, the San Diego *Sun*, and other publications. He is the director of over 25 motion pictures, including Park Row, Forty Guns, and The Crimson Kimono. His novels include The Dark Page and La grande meleé.

Loren Ghiglione is the Editor of *The News* in Southbridge, Massachusetts. A past President of the American Society of Newspaper Editors, he has been a visiting Professor at the Graduate School of Journalism, Columbia University; organized the Library of Congress's travelling exhibition on the newspaper in popular culture; and has published widely on the history of journalism, including The American Journalist: Paradox of the Press and The Buying and Selling of America's Newspapers.

Jeffrey Richards is Professor of Cultural History at the University of Lancaster and author of numerous books on the cinema including The Age of the Dream Palace: Cinema and Society in Britain 1930 - 1939; Thorold Dickinson: The Man and His Films; Visions of Yesterday; and (with Tony Aldgate) Best of British: Cinema and Society 1930 - 1970.

Deac Rossell was film editor of the Boston *Phoenix* and has written for *Esquire* magazine, the Boston *Globe*, *American Film*, and other publications. The former National Special Projects Officer for the Directors Guild of America, he is currently Head of Programme Planning for the National Film Theatre, London.

ACKNOWLEDGEMENTS

The editors would like to most gratefully acknowledge the help and advice of our colleague contributors to this volume for their timely advice and expertise, and in addition thank Kersti French for translation, Karl French for additions to the filmography, Liz Balcon and Desmond Balmer of The Observer for support and enthusiasm, John Harmer for design of the dossier, Michel Ciment for advice, Philip Goodfellow of KPC for guidance, and the Programme Planning, Technical, Publicity, and House staffs of the National Film Theatre who made certain that the movies reached the screen and the public.

Portions of the filmography and an earlier version of Deac Rossell's essay were first published in Questioning Media Ethics, edited by Bernard Rubin (New York, 1976: Praeger Publishers), and appreciative acknowledgement is made to Bernard Rubin and the Institute of Democratic Communication at Boston University.

Sam Fuller generously allowed the reprinting of his essay originally commissioned for a 1975 Season at the Museum of Fine Arts, Boston.

Loren Ghiglione gave permission for the re-use of a chapter of The American Journalist: Paradox of the Press (Washington, 1990: The Library of Congress).

Excerpts from pages 40-45 from The Hollywood Social Problem Film are Copyright © 1981 by Peter Roffman and Jim Purdy. Reprinted by permission of Indiana University Press.

The editors also particularly acknowledge the work and the daily struggles of those professional journalists whose work, whether for the papers or the films, is represented in the films shown and unshown, directly or indirectly, and of the issues they grapple with on a practical level whilst working to inexorable deadlines.

P.F / D.R.